Letts

GCSE
Success

Revision Guide

AQA
Chemistry

Christine Horbury

Contents

Revised

Contents

Unit 3

N.B. The numbers in brackets correspond to the reference numbers on the AQA GCSE Chemistry specification.

How to Use This Guide

This revision guide has been written and developed to help you get the most out of your revision.

This guide covers both Foundation and Higher Tier content.

HT Content that will only be tested on the Higher Tier papers appears in a pale yellow tinted box labelled with the **HT** symbol.

- The **coloured page headers** clearly identify the separate units, so that you can revise for each one separately: Unit 1 is red; Unit 2 is purple, and Unit 3 is blue.
- The exam will include questions on **How Science Works**, so make sure you work through the How Science Works section in green at the front of this guide before each exam.
- There are two **summary pages** at the end of each unit, which outline all the key points. These are great for a final recap before your exam.

- There are **practice questions** at the end of each unit so you can test yourself on what you've just learned. (The answers are given on p.92–93 so you can mark your own answers.)
- You'll find **key words** in a yellow box on each 2-page spread. They are also highlighted in colour within the text; higher tier key words are highlighted in a different colour. Make sure you know and understand all these words before moving on!
- There's a **glossary** at the back of the book. It contains all the key words that appear throughout the book so you can check any definitions you're unsure of.
- The **tick boxes** on the contents page let you track your revision progress: simply put a tick in the box next to each topic when you're confident that you know it.
- Don't just read the guide – **learn actively**! Constantly test yourself without looking at the text.

Good luck with your exam!

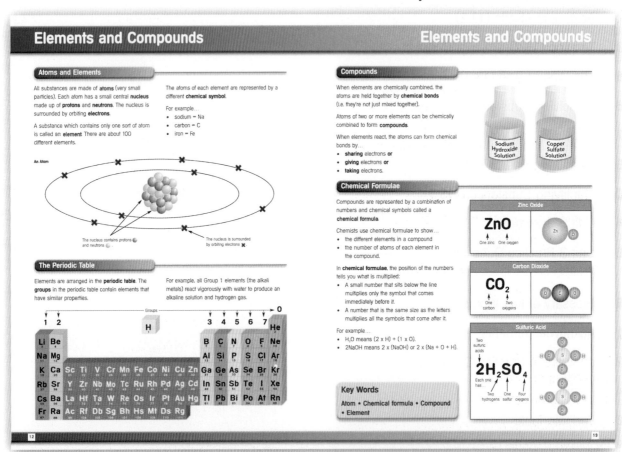

How Science Works – Explanation

The AQA GCSE science specifications incorporate:

1. **Science Content** – all the scientific explanations and evidence that you need to know for the exams. (It is covered on pages 12–87 of this revision guide.)

2. **How Science Works** – a set of key concepts, relevant to all areas of science. It covers…
   - the relationship between scientific evidence, and scientific explanations and theories
   - how scientific evidence is collected
   - how reliable and valid scientific evidence is
   - the role of science in society
   - the impact science has on our lives
   - how decisions are made about the ways science and technology are used in different situations, and the factors affecting these decisions.

Your teacher(s) will have taught these two types of content together in your science lessons. Likewise, the questions on your exam papers will probably combine elements from both types of content. So, to answer them, you'll need to recall the relevant scientific facts *and* apply your knowledge of how science works.

The key concepts of How Science Works are summarised in this section of the revision guide (pages 6–11).

You should be familiar with all of these concepts. If there is anything you are unsure about, ask your teacher to explain it to you.

How Science Works is designed to help you learn about and understand the practical side of science. It aims to help you develop your skills when it comes to…
- evaluating information
- developing arguments
- drawing conclusions.

N.B. Practical tips on how to evaluate information are included on page 11.

How Science Works

Science attempts to explain the world we live in.

Scientists carry out investigations and collect evidence in order to…

- **explain phenomena** (i.e. how and why things happen)
- **solve problems**.

Scientific knowledge and understanding can lead to the **development of new technologies** (e.g. in medicine and industry), which have a huge impact on…

- society
- the environment.

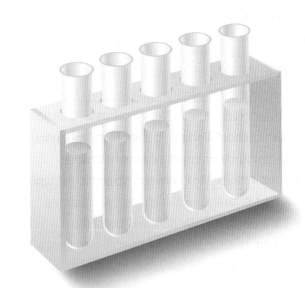

What is the Purpose of Evidence?

Scientific evidence provides **facts** which answer a specific question and either **support** or **disprove** an idea / theory.

Evidence is often based on data that has been collected through…

- **observations**
- **measurements**.

To allow scientists to reach conclusions, evidence must be…

- **reliable** – it must be trustworthy
- **valid** – it must be reliable and answer the question.

N.B. If data isn't reliable, it can't be valid.

To ensure scientific evidence is reliable and valid, scientists use ideas and practices relating to…

1. observations
2. investigations
3. measurements
4. data presentation
5. conclusions.

These five key ideas are covered in more detail on the following pages.

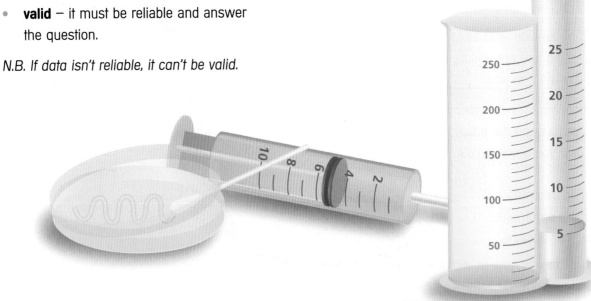

Observations

Most scientific investigations begin with an **observation**. A scientist observes an event / phenomenon and decides to find out more about how and why it happens.

The first step is to develop a **hypothesis** to suggest an explanation for the phenomenon. Hypotheses normally suggest a relationship between two or more **variables** (factors that change). Hypotheses are based on…
* careful observations
* existing scientific knowledge
* a bit of creative thinking.

The hypothesis is used to make a **prediction**, which can be tested through scientific investigation. The data collected from the investigation will…
* support the hypothesis **or**
* show it to be untrue **or**
* lead to the development of a new hypothesis.

If new observations or data don't match existing explanations or theories, they must be checked for reliability and validity.

Sometimes, if the new observations and data are valid, existing theories and explanations have to be revised or amended, and so scientific knowledge grows and develops.

Example

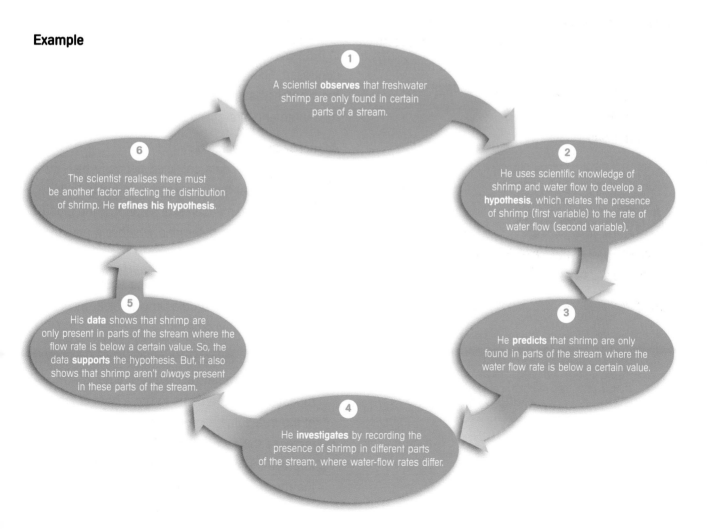

1 A scientist **observes** that freshwater shrimp are only found in certain parts of a stream.

2 He uses scientific knowledge of shrimp and water flow to develop a **hypothesis**, which relates the presence of shrimp (first variable) to the rate of water flow (second variable).

3 He **predicts** that shrimp are only found in parts of the stream where the water flow rate is below a certain value.

4 He **investigates** by recording the presence of shrimp in different parts of the stream, where water-flow rates differ.

5 His **data** shows that shrimp are only present in parts of the stream where the flow rate is below a certain value. So, the data **supports** the hypothesis. But, it also shows that shrimp aren't *always* present in these parts of the stream.

6 The scientist realises there must be another factor affecting the distribution of shrimp. He **refines his hypothesis**.

How Science Works

An **investigation** involves collecting data to find out whether there is a relationship between two **variables**. A variable is a factor that can take different values.

In an investigation there are two variables:

1. **Independent variable** – can be adjusted (changed) by the person carrying out the investigation.
2. **Dependent variable** – measured each time a change is made to the independent variable, to see if it also changes.

Variables can have different types of values:

- **Continuous variables** – take numerical values. These are usually measurements, e.g. temperature.
- **Discrete variables** – only take whole-number values. These are usually quantities, e.g. the number of shrimp in a stream.
- **Ordered variables** – have relative values, e.g. 'small', 'medium' or 'large'.
- **Categoric variables** – have a limited number of specific values, e.g. different breeds of dog.

N.B. Numerical values tend to be more informative than ordered and categoric variables.

An investigation tries to find out whether an **observed** link between two variables is…

- **causal** – a change in one variable causes a change in the other
- **due to association** – the changes in the two variables are linked by a third variable
- **due to chance** – the change in the two variables is unrelated; it is coincidental.

Fair Tests

In a **fair test**, the only factor that can affect the dependent variable is the independent variable. Other **outside variables** that could influence the results are kept the same or eliminated.

It's a lot easier to carry out a fair test in the lab than in the field, where conditions can't always be controlled. The impact of an outside variable, like the weather, has to be reduced by ensuring all measurements are affected by it in the same way.

Accuracy and Precision

How accurate the data collected needs to be depends on what the investigation is trying to find out. For example, measures of alcohol in the blood must be accurate to determine whether a person is legally fit to drive.

The data collected must be **precise** enough to form a **valid conclusion**: it should provide clear evidence for or against the hypothesis.

To ensure data is as accurate as possible, you can…

- calculate the **mean** (average) of a set of repeated measurements to get a **best estimate** of the true value
- increase the number of measurements taken to improve the **accuracy** and the **reliability** of the mean.

Measurements

Apart from outside variables, there are a number of factors that can affect the reliability and validity of measurements:

- **Accuracy of instruments** – depends on how accurately the instrument has been calibrated. (Expensive equipment is usually more accurately calibrated.)
- **Sensitivity of instruments** – determined by the smallest change in value that the instrument can detect. For example, bathroom scales aren't sensitive enough to detect the changes in a baby's weight, but the scales used by a midwife are.

- **Human error** – can occur if you lose concentration. Systematic (repeated) errors can occur if the instrument hasn't been calibrated properly or is misused.

You need to examine any **anomalous** (irregular) values to try to determine why they appear. If they have been caused by an equipment failure or human error, it is common practice to discount them from any calculations.

Presenting Data

Data is often presented in a **chart** or **graph** because it makes...

- the patterns more evident
- it easier to see the relationship between two variables.

The relationship between variables can be...

- **linear** (positive or negative), **or**
- **directly proportional**.

If you present data clearly, it is easier to identify any anomalous values. The type of chart or graph you use to present data depends on the type of variable involved:

1. **Tables** organise data (but patterns and anomalies aren't always obvious).
2. **Bar charts** display data when the independent variable is categoric or discrete and the dependent variable is continuous.
3. **Line graphs** display data when both variables are continuous.
4. **Scattergrams** (scatter diagrams) show the underlying relationship between two variables. This can be made clearer if you include a **line of best fit**.

1.

Height (cm)	127	165	149	147	155	161	154	138	145
Shoe Size	5	8	5	6	5	5	6	4	5

2.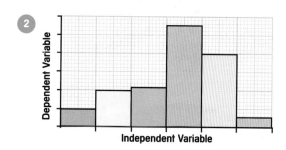

3.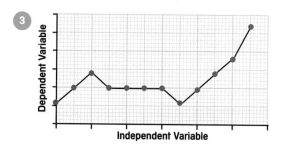

4.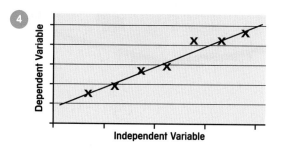

How Science Works

Conclusions **should**…
- describe the patterns and relationships between variables
- take all the data into account
- make direct reference to the original hypothesis / prediction.

Conclusions **shouldn't**…
- be influenced by anything other than the data collected
- disregard any data (except anomalous values)
- include any speculation.

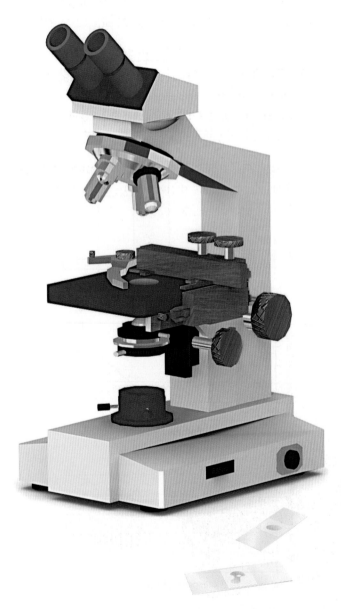

Evaluation

An **evaluation** looks at the whole investigation. It should consider…
- the original purpose of the investigation
- the appropriateness of the methods and techniques used
- the reliability and validity of the data
- the validity of the conclusions.

The **reliability** of an investigation can be increased by…
- looking at relevant data from secondary sources
- using an alternative method to check results
- ensuring that the results can be reproduced by others.

Science and Society

Scientific understanding can lead to technological developments. These developments can be exploited by different groups of people for different reasons. For example, the successful development of a new drug…
- benefits the drugs company financially
- improves the quality of life for patients.

Scientific developments can raise certain **issues**. An issue is an important question that is in dispute and needs to be settled. The resolution of an issue may not be based on scientific evidence alone.

There are several different **issues** which can arise:
- **Social** – the impact on the human population of a community, city, country, or the world.
- **Economic** – money and related factors like employment and the distribution of resources.
- **Environmental** – the impact on the planet, its natural ecosystems and resources.
- **Ethical** – what is morally right and wrong; requires a valued judgement to be made about what is acceptable.

N.B. There is often an overlap between social and economic issues.

Evaluating Information

It is important to be able to evaluate information relating to social-scientific issues, both for the exam and to help you make informed decisions in life.

When evaluating information...
- make a list of **pluses**
- make a list of **minuses**
- consider how each point might **impact on society**.

*N.B. Remember, **PMI** – **p**luses, **m**inuses, **i**mpact on society.*

You also need to consider whether the source of information is reliable and credible. Some important factors to consider are...
- **opinions**
- **bias**
- **weight of evidence**.

Opinions are personal viewpoints. Opinions backed up by valid and reliable evidence carry far more weight than those based on non-scientific ideas.

Information is **biased** if it favours one particular viewpoint without providing a balanced account. Biased information might include incomplete evidence or try to influence how you interpret the evidence.

Scientific evidence can be given **undue weight** or dismissed too lightly due to...
- political significance
- status (academic or professional status, experience, authority and reputation).

Limitations of Science

Although science can help us in lots of ways, it can't supply all the answers. We are still finding out about things and developing our scientific knowledge.

There are some questions that science can't answer. These tend to be questions relating to...
- ethical issues
- situations where it isn't possible to collect reliable and valid scientific evidence.

Science can often tell us if something **can** be done, and **how** it should be done, but it can't tell us whether it **should** be done.

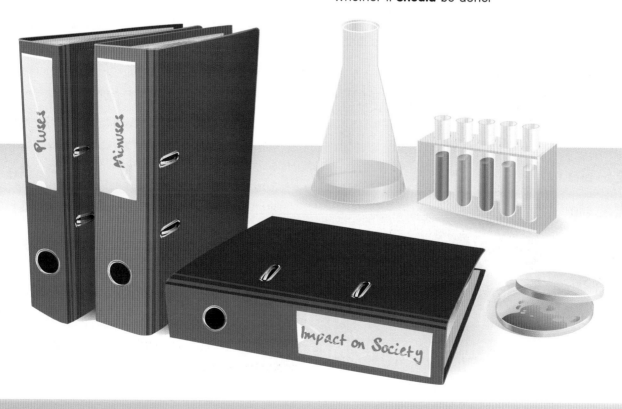

Elements and Compounds

Atoms and Elements

All substances are made of **atoms** (very small particles). Each atom has a small central **nucleus** made up of **protons** and **neutrons**. The nucleus is surrounded by orbiting **electrons**.

A substance which contains only one sort of atom is called an **element**. There are about 100 different elements.

The atoms of each element are represented by a different **chemical symbol**.

For example…
- sodium = Na
- carbon = C
- iron = Fe

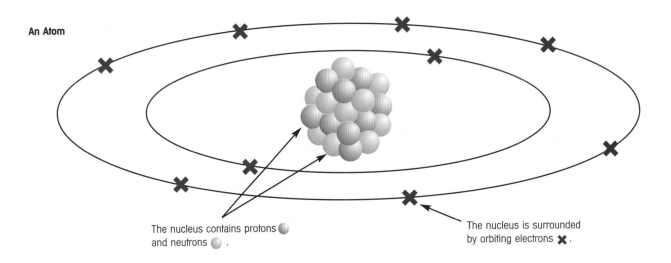

An Atom

The nucleus contains protons and neutrons .

The nucleus is surrounded by orbiting electrons ✖ .

The Periodic Table

Elements are arranged in the **periodic table**. The **groups** in the periodic table contain elements that have similar properties.

For example, all Group 1 elements (the alkali metals) react vigorously with water to produce an alkaline solution and hydrogen gas.

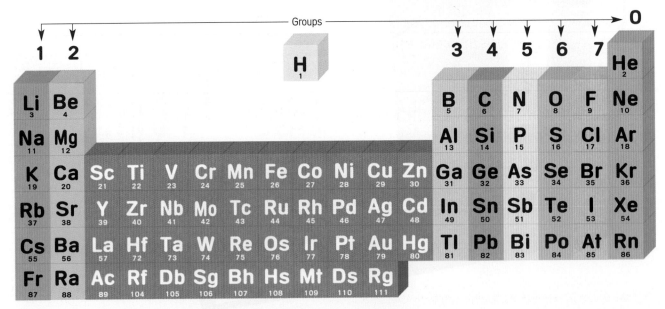

Elements and Compounds

Compounds

When elements are chemically combined, the atoms are held together by **chemical bonds** (i.e. they're not just mixed together).

Atoms of two or more elements can be chemically combined to form **compounds**.

When elements react, the atoms can form chemical bonds by…
- **sharing** electrons **or**
- **giving** electrons **or**
- **taking** electrons.

Sodium Hydroxide Solution

Copper Sulfate Solution

Chemical Formulae

Compounds are represented by a combination of numbers and chemical symbols called a **chemical formula**.

Chemists use chemical formulae to show…
- the different elements in a compound
- the number of atoms of each element in the compound.

In **chemical formulae**, the position of the numbers tells you what is multiplied:
- A small number that sits below the line multiplies only the symbol that comes immediately before it.
- A number that is the same size as the letters multiplies all the symbols that come after it.

For example…
- H_2O means $(2 \times H) + (1 \times O)$.
- $2NaOH$ means $2 \times (NaOH)$ or $2 \times (Na + O + H)$.

Zinc Oxide

ZnO

One zinc   One oxygen

Zn   O

Carbon Dioxide

CO$_2$

One carbon   Two oxygens

O   C   O

Sulfuric Acid

Two sulfuric acids

2H$_2$SO$_4$

Each one has…

Two hydrogens   One sulfur   Four oxygens

O
H O S O H
O

O

O
H O S O H
O

Key Words

Atom • Chemical formula • Compound • Element

Chemical Reactions

Chemical Reactions

You can show what has happened during a **chemical reaction** by writing a **word equation**.

The **reactants** (i.e. the substances that react) are on one side of the equation and the **products** (i.e. the new substances that are formed) are on the other.

The total mass of the products of a chemical reaction is always equal to the total mass of the reactants. This is because **no atoms are lost or made**: the products of a chemical reaction are made up from exactly the same atoms as the reactants.

So, chemical symbol equations must always be **balanced**: there must be the same number of atoms of each element on the reactant side of the equation as there is on the product side.

Number of atoms of each element on products side	=	Number of atoms of each element on reactants side

Example

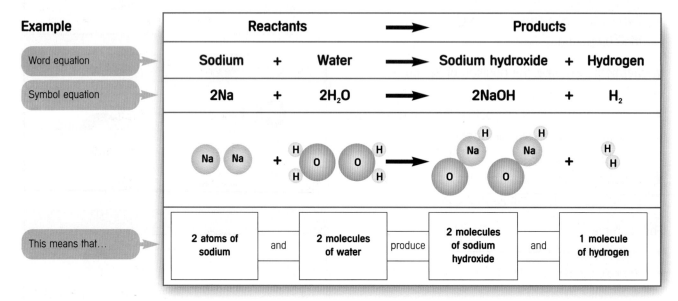

	Reactants	→	Products
Word equation	Sodium + Water	→	Sodium hydroxide + Hydrogen
Symbol equation	$2Na$ + $2H_2O$	→	$2NaOH$ + H_2

This means that...

2 atoms of sodium	and	2 molecules of water	produce	2 molecules of sodium hydroxide	and	1 molecule of hydrogen

Key Words

Atom • Chemical reaction • Product • Reactant

Writing Balanced Equations

The following steps tell you how to write a balanced equation.

1. Write a word equation for the chemical reaction.
2. Substitute in formulae for the elements or compounds.
3. Balance the equation by adding numbers in front of the reactants and / or products.
4. Write down the balanced symbol equation.

Reactants			$\longrightarrow$	Products
Magnesium	+	**Oxygen**	$\longrightarrow$	**Magnesium oxide**
Mg	+	O_2	$\longrightarrow$	**MgO**

1 — Write a word equation

2 — Substitute in formulae

3 — Balance the equation

- There are two **O**s on the reactant side, but only one **O** on the product side. We need to add another **MgO** to the product side to balance the **O**s.
- We now need to add another **Mg** on the reactant side to balance the **Mg**s.
- There are two magnesium atoms and two oxygen atoms on each side – **it is balanced**.

4 — Write a balanced symbol equation

2Mg	+	O_2	$\longrightarrow$	**2MgO**

Reactants			$\longrightarrow$	Products
Nitrogen	+	**Hydrogen**	$\longrightarrow$	**Ammonia**
N_2	+	H_2	$\longrightarrow$	NH_3

1 — Write a word equation

2 — Substitute in formulae

3 — Balance the equation

- There are two **N**s on the reactant side, but only one **N** on the product side. We need to add another **NH₃** to the product side to balance the **N**s.
- We now need to add two more **H₂**s on the reactant side to balance the **H₂**s.
- There are two nitrogen atoms and six hydrogen atoms on each side – **it is balanced**.

4 — Write a balanced symbol equation

N_2	+	$3H_2$	$\longrightarrow$	$2NH_3$

Limestone

Limestone (CaCO₃)

- Limestone is a **sedimentary rock**.
- It consists mainly of **calcium carbonate**.
- It is cheap, easy to obtain and has many uses.

Limestone can be used…
- as a building material
- for producing slaked lime
- for making glass
- for making cement, mortar and concrete.

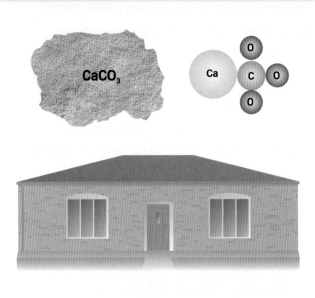

As a building material – Limestone can be quarried, cut into blocks and used to build houses. It can be **eroded** by **acid rain** but this is a very slow process.

Producing slaked lime – When calcium carbonate is heated in a kiln it **decomposes**. This reaction is called **thermal decomposition**. It causes the calcium carbonate to break down into calcium oxide (quicklime) and carbon dioxide. The calcium oxide can then be reacted (**slaked**) with water to produce **slaked lime** (calcium hydroxide). Slaked lime can be used to neutralise soils and lakes, preventing crop failure. Carbonates of other metals decompose in a similar way when they are heated.

Making glass – Powdered limestone is mixed with sand and sodium carbonate and heated. When it cools, it is transparent.

Making cement, mortar and concrete – Powdered limestone is roasted in a rotary kiln with powdered clay to produce dry **cement**. When sand and water are mixed in, **mortar** is produced. Mortar is used to hold bricks and stones together. When gravel, sand and water are mixed in, **concrete** is produced.

Key Words

Alloy • Atom • Chemical reaction • Compound • Decompose • Element • Minerals • Ore • Reduction • Sedimentary rock

Ores

The Earth's crust contains many naturally occurring **elements** and **compounds** called **minerals**.

A **metal ore** is a mineral which contains enough metal to make it economically viable to extract it. This can change over time; there may come a time when it isn't worth spending money to extract it.

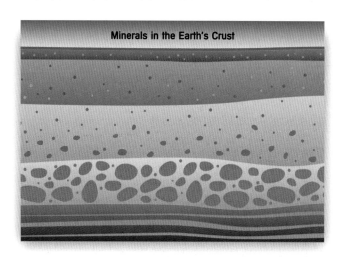

Minerals in the Earth's Crust

Extracting Metals from their Ores

The method of extraction depends on **how reactive the metal is**.

Unreactive metals like gold exist naturally in the Earth and can be obtained through panning. But, most metals are found as **metal oxides**, or as compounds that can be easily changed into a metal oxide.

- To extract a metal from its oxide, the oxygen must be removed by heating the oxide with another element in a **chemical reaction**. This process is called **reduction**.
- Metals that are **less reactive than carbon** can be extracted from their oxides by heating with carbon, e.g. iron, lead.

Iron

Iron oxide can be reduced in a blast furnace to produce **iron**. Molten iron obtained from a blast furnace contains roughly…
- 96% iron
- 4% carbon and other metals.

Because it is impure, the iron is very brittle with limited uses. To produce pure iron, all the **impurities** have to be removed.

The **atoms** in pure iron are arranged in layers, which can slide over each other easily. This makes pure iron soft and malleable − it can be easily shaped. But it's too soft for many practical uses.

The properties of iron can be changed by mixing it with small quantities of carbon or other metals to make **steel**. A majority of iron is converted into steel. Steel is an **alloy**.

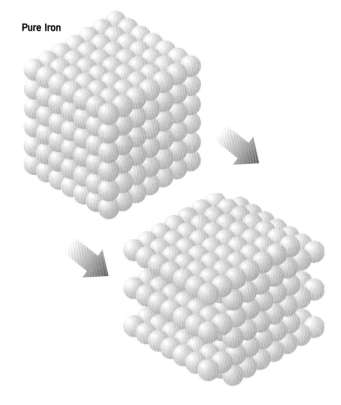

Pure Iron

Metals

Alloys

An **alloy** is a mixture which contains a **metal** and at least one other **element**.

The added element disturbs the regular arrangement of the metal atoms so the layers don't slide over each other so easily.

Alloys are, therefore, usually stronger and harder than pure metal.

Many of the metals you come across everyday are alloys. Pure copper, gold and aluminium are too soft for many uses. They are mixed with small amounts of similar metals to make them harder for items in everyday use, for example, coins.

Steel

Carbon is added to iron to make the alloy **steel**.

Alloys like steel are developed to have the necessary properties for a specific purpose.

In steel, the amount of carbon and / or other elements determines its properties:
- Steel with a high carbon content is hard and strong.
- Steel with a low carbon content is soft and easily shaped.
- **Stainless steel** is hard and resistant to corrosion.

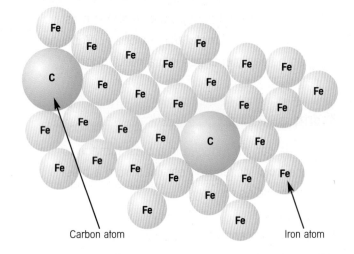

Carbon atom   Iron atom

Smart Alloys

Smart alloys belong to a group of materials that are being developed to meet the demands of modern engineering and manufacturing. These materials respond to changes in their environment.

Smart alloys **remember their shape**. They can be deformed, but will return to their original shape, for example, flexible spectacle frames.

The Transition Metals

Between Groups 2 and 3 in the Periodic Table is a block of metallic elements called the **transition metals**.

The transition metals…

- are good **conductors** of heat and electricity
- are hard and mechanically strong
- have high melting points (except mercury)
- can be bent or hammered into shape.

These properties make the transition metals very useful as structural materials, and as electrical and thermal conductors.

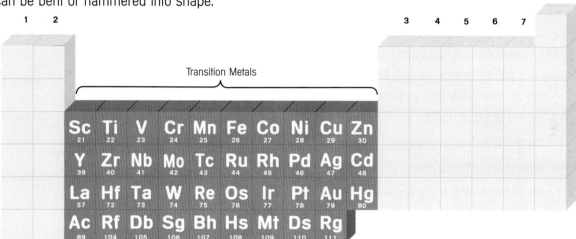

Extracting Transition Metals

Copper and **aluminium** are extracted from their ores by **electrolysis**. Electrolysis has many stages and requires a lot of energy, making it an expensive process. Extracting **titanium** is also very expensive.

Copper is useful for electrical wiring and plumbing. But, natural supplies of ores containing large quantities of copper are limited.

Scientists are trying to find ways to extract copper from other low-grade ores to limit damage to the environment caused by traditional copper mining.

Aluminium is resistant to corrosion and has a low density so it is very light. It is used for…

- drinks cans
- window frames
- lightweight vehicles
- aeroplanes.

Titanium is strong and resistant to corrosion. It is used in…

- aeroplanes
- nuclear reactors
- replacement hip joints.

Recycling Metals

Metals should be **recycled** wherever possible to…

- save money and energy
- make sure all the natural resources aren't used up
- reduce the damaging impact on the environment.

Key Words

Alloy • Conductor • Electrolysis • Element • Smart alloy

Crude Oil and Hydrocarbons

Crude Oil

Crude oil on its own isn't very useful. But it is a **mixture** of compounds, some of which are very useful.

A **mixture** consists of two or more elements or compounds which are **not chemically combined** together. The properties of the substances in a mixture remain unchanged, so they can be separated by physical methods, such as **distillation**.

Most of the compounds in crude oil consist of molecules made up of only **carbon** and **hydrogen** atoms. These compounds are called **hydrocarbons**. **Hydrocarbon** molecules vary in size. This affects their properties and how they are used as fuels.

The larger the hydrocarbon (i.e. the more carbon and hydrogen atoms in a molecule)…
- the less easily it flows (it's more viscous)
- the higher its boiling point
- the less volatile it is
- the less easily it ignites.

Long-Chain Hydrocarbon	Short-Chain Hydrocarbons

Fractional Distillation

Crude oil can be separated into different **fractions** (parts) by **fractional distillation.**

1. The crude oil is evaporated (by heating).
2. It is allowed to condense at a range of different temperatures.
3. It then forms fractions.

Each fraction contains hydrocarbon molecules with a similar number of carbon atoms. Most of the hydrocarbons obtained are **alkanes** (**saturated hydrocarbons**).

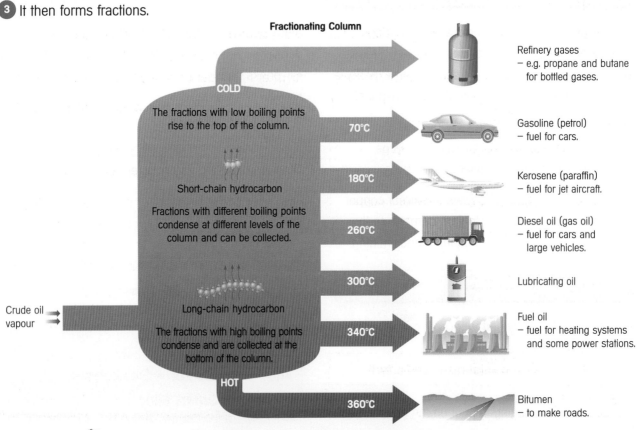

Fractionating Column

COLD

The fractions with low boiling points rise to the top of the column.

Short-chain hydrocarbon

Fractions with different boiling points condense at different levels of the column and can be collected.

Long-chain hydrocarbon

The fractions with high boiling points condense and are collected at the bottom of the column.

HOT

Crude oil vapour →

Refinery gases
– e.g. propane and butane for bottled gases.

70°C — Gasoline (petrol)
– fuel for cars.

180°C — Kerosene (paraffin)
– fuel for jet aircraft.

260°C — Diesel oil (gas oil)
– fuel for cars and large vehicles.

300°C — Lubricating oil

340°C — Fuel oil
– fuel for heating systems and some power stations.

360°C — Bitumen
– to make roads.

Crude Oil and Hydrocarbons

Alkanes (Saturated Hydrocarbons)

The 'spine' of a hydrocarbon is made up of a chain of carbon atoms. When these are joined together by **single carbon carbon bonds** the hydrocarbon is **saturated** and is known as an **alkane**.

- Hydrogen atoms can make 1 bond each.
- Carbon atoms can make 4 bonds each.
- The simplest alkane, **methane**, is made up of 4 hydrogen atoms and 1 carbon atom.

The general formula for alkanes is C_nH_{2n+2}.

The carbon atoms in alkenes are linked to 4 other atoms by **single bonds**. This means that the alkane is saturated. This explains why alkanes are fairly unreactive, but they do burn well.

The shorter-chain hydrocarbons release energy more quickly by burning, so there is greater demand for them as **fuels**.

Alkanes can be represented like this:

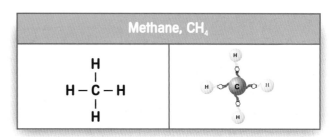

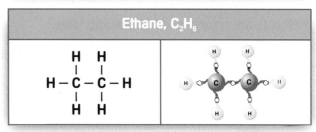

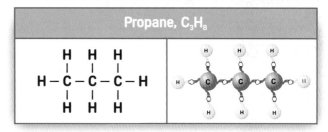

Burning Fuels

Most **fuels** contain carbon and hydrogen. Many also contain **sulfur**. As fuels burn they produce waste products, which are released into the atmosphere:

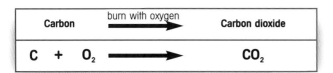

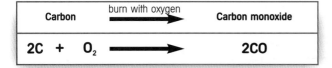

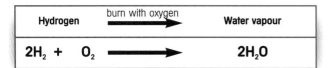

Sulfur	burn with oxygen →	Sulfur dioxide
S + O_2	→	SO_2

For example, the fuel ethane (C_2H_6) burns to produce carbon dioxide (from the carbon in the ethane) and water (from the hydrogen in the ethane).

- Carbon dioxide causes **global warming** due to the greenhouse effect.
- Particles cause **global dimming**.
- Sulfur dioxide causes **acid rain**.

Sulfur can be removed from fuel before burning (e.g. in motor vehicles). Sulfur dioxide can be removed from the waste gases after **combustion** (e.g. in power stations). But both of these processes add to the cost.

Key Words

Alkane • Crude oil • Distillation • Fractional distillation • Fuel • Hydrocarbon

Unit 1a Summary

Atoms and Elements

All substances are made of atoms:

Proton ● in the nucleus

Neutron ● in the nucleus

Orbiting electron ✖

An element = A substance that contains only one sort of atom.

Elements are arranged in the **periodic table**.

A compound = A substance that contains two or more elements chemically combined.

Compounds are represented by chemical formulae, e.g. CO_2 — Two oxygens

One carbon

Chemical Reactions

Number of atoms of each element in **products** = Number of atoms of each element in **reactants**.

Balanced Equations

Write a word equation → Write in formulae → Add numbers to balance equation → Write balanced symbol equation

Limestone

Limestone = Mainly calcium carbonate = $CaCO_3$.

Limestone can be used...

- for building
- to make glass
- to make cement, mortar and concrete.
- to produce slaked lime:

thermal decomposition of calcium carbonate ⇒ quicklime + CO_2

When quicklime is slaked with water ⇒ slaked lime produced

Ores and Alloys

Metal ores = **Minerals** found in Earth's crust which contain enough metal to make it worthwhile extracting it.

Extraction method depends on reactivity of metal.

Most metals are found as oxides. Oxygen must be removed by **reduction** to obtain metal, e.g. iron oxide is reduced to produce iron.

Iron can be mixed with carbon or other metals to make the alloy steel.

Alloy = A mixture containing a metal and at least one other element.

Smart alloy = A material that responds to changes in its environment.

Transition Metals

Transition metals…
- are good conductors
- are hard and strong
- have high melting points
- can be bent / hammered into shape.

Copper and aluminium are extracted from their ores by **electrolysis** – an expensive process. Extracting titanium is also expensive.

Metals should be recycled whenever possible to save energy and money, reduce damage to the environment and prevent all natural resources being used up.

Crude Oil

Crude oil = A mixture of compounds made up of carbon and hydrogen atoms.

Crude oil is separated into fractions by **fractional distillation**:

Crude oil is evaporated ➡ It is allowed to condense ➡ It forms fractions (mostly alkanes)

Alkanes (Saturated Hydrocarbons)

Carbon atoms in a hydrocarbon are joined by single bonds = saturated hydrocarbon = alkane, e.g.

Methane, CH_4
H | H – C – H | H

General formula for alkanes = C_nH_{2n+2}

Burning Fuels

Most fuels contain carbon and hydrogen. Many contain sulfur too. They release waste products when burned.

Element in Fuel	Waste Product Released	Effect of Waste Product
Carbon	Carbon dioxide	Causes global warming.
	Carbon monoxide	Particles cause global dimming.
Hydrogen	Water vapour	None
Sulfur	Sulfur dioxide	Causes acid rain.

Unit 1a Practice Questions

1 Match the words A, B, C and D with the spaces numbered 1 to 4 in the sentences below.

A formula ....

B atoms ....

C compounds ....

D bonds ....

All substances are made of particles called __1__ . These particles can join with others to form __2__ in which they are held together by chemical __3__ . The number and type of particles which are joined together can be represented by a chemical __4__ of the substance.

2 This question has three parts. For each part, put a tick next to the correct answer.

a) Limestone contains the compound…

  i) calcium oxide

  ii) calcium carbonate

  iii) calcium hydroxide

  iv) calcium sulfate

b) The products formed by the thermal decomposition of limestone are…

  i) slaked lime and carbon dioxide

  ii) slaked lime and carbon monoxide

  iii) quicklime and carbon monoxide

  iv) quicklime and carbon dioxide

c) The common name for calcium hydroxide is…

  i) slaked lime

  ii) quicklime

  iii) limestone

  iv) lime

3 Match the metals A, B, C and D with the descriptions numbered 1 to 4 below.

A titanium (Ti) ....

B copper (Cu) ....

C iron (Fe) ....

D aluminium (Al) ....

1 It is used to make the alloy steel.
2 It is used to make replacement hip joints.
3 It is strong and light and will not rust.
4 It is a good conductor of heat and electricity.

4 Explain why gold doesn't need to be extracted by methods used for other metals.

....

5 Lead is extracted from the compound lead oxide by the process of reduction.

a) Describe the process.

....

b) Why is this process used for this metal?

....

6 a) What process is used for the extraction of aluminium? ....

b) Why isn't the process of reduction used?

....

7 Give two reasons why metals should be recycled whenever possible.

a) .... **b)** ....

8 Match the words A, B, C and D with the spaces numbered 1 to 4 in the sentences below.

A high .... **B** low ....

C condensed .... **D** vaporised ....

During the fractional distillation of crude oil, the oil is first ....**1**.... and then the fractions are ....**2**.... . The fractions with ....**3**.... boiling points are collected at the top of the fractionating column. Bitumen has a ....**4**.... boiling point.

9 The alkane ethane C_2H_6 is a hydrocarbon fuel.

Draw a structural formula diagram to illustrate its carbon–hydrogen bonds.

10 How will an alkane with more carbon atoms in its molecule be different from ethane in its…

a) boiling point? ....

b) viscosity? ....

11 a) What would be the products of burning pure ethane?

....

b) If sulfur was present in an impure form of this fuel, which additional product would be made?

....

c) Write a balanced symbol equation for this reaction.

....

Cracking Hydrocarbons

Cracking Hydrocarbons

Longer-chain hydrocarbons can be **cracked** (broken down) into shorter, more useful chains, which release energy more quickly by burning.

heat + catalyst
Long-chain hydrocarbon ➡ **Short-chain hydrocarbons**

Cracking involves…
- heating the hydrocarbons until they vaporise
- passing the vapour over a hot **catalyst**.

A **thermal decomposition** reaction then takes place.

The products of cracking include **alkanes** and **alkenes** (**unsaturated hydrocarbons**). Some of the products are useful as fuels.

Cracking Hydrocarbons in the Laboratory

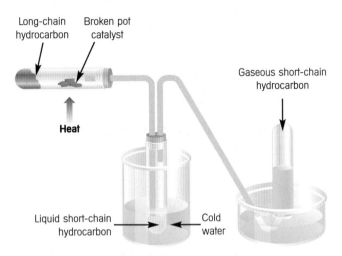

Long-chain hydrocarbon · Broken pot catalyst

Heat

Gaseous short-chain hydrocarbon

Liquid short-chain hydrocarbon · Cold water

Alkenes (Unsaturated Hydrocarbons)

As well as forming single bonds with other atoms, carbon atoms can form **double bonds**. This means that not all the carbon atoms are linked to 4 other atoms; a **double carbon carbon bond** is present instead.

Some of the products of cracking are hydrocarbon molecules with at least one double bond (alkenes).
- The general formula for alkenes is C_nH_{2n}.
- The simplest alkene is ethene, C_2H_4.
- Ethene is made up of 4 hydrogen atoms and 2 carbon atoms, and contains one double carbon carbon bond.

Alkenes can be represented using displayed formulae:

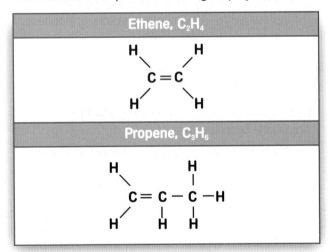

Ethene, C_2H_4

Propene, C_3H_6

Making Alcohol from Ethene

Ethanol is an alcohol. It can be produced by reacting the alkene **ethene** with steam in the presence of a **catalyst**, phosphoric acid.

		phosphoric acid	
Ethene	**+ Steam**	➡	**Ethanol**

Polymerisation

Because alkenes are unsaturated (i.e. not fully occupied – they have a double bond), they are useful for making other molecules, especially **polymers** (long-chain molecules).

Small alkene molecules (**monomers**) join together to form polymers. This is **polymerisation**.

Polymers such as **poly(ethene)** and **poly(propene)** are made in this way.

The properties of polymers depend on...
- what they are made from
- the conditions under which they are made.

For example, slime with different **viscosities** can be made from poly(ethenol). The viscosity of the slime depends on the temperature and concentrations of the poly(ethenol) and borax from which it is made.

The materials commonly called **plastics** are all synthetic polymers.

1 The small alkene molecules are called monomers.

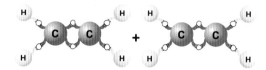

2 Their double bonds are easily broken.

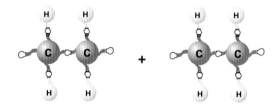

3 Large numbers of molecules can therefore be joined in this way.

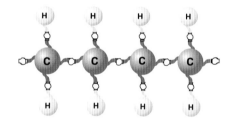

Representing Polymerisation

Polymerisation can be represented like this:

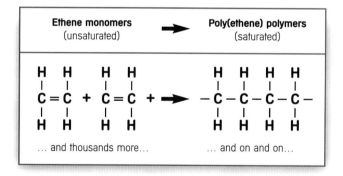

Ethene monomers (unsaturated)	→	Poly(ethene) polymers (saturated)

... and thousands more...   ... and on and on...

The general formula for polymerisation can be used to represent the formation of any simple polymer:

$$n \left(\begin{array}{c} | \ | \\ C = C \\ | \ | \end{array} \right) \longrightarrow \left(\begin{array}{c} | \ | \\ C - C \\ | \ | \end{array} \right)_n$$

where n is a very large number

Key Words

Alkane • Alkene • Catalyst • Cracking • Polymer • Polymerisation

Oils and Emulsions

Hydrogenation

Generally, the more double carbon carbon bonds there are in a substance, the lower its melting point.

So, **unsaturated fats** (oils) tend to have melting points below room temperature.

The melting point of an oil can be raised above room temperature by removing some or all of its carbon carbon bonds. This hardens the oil into a solid fat, for example, margarine which can be spread on your bread or used for making cakes and pastries.

This process is called **hydrogenation**.

1 The **unsaturated fat (oil)** is heated with **hydrogen** at about 60°C, in the presence of a **nickel catalyst**.

2 A reaction takes place which **removes the double carbon carbon bonds** to produce a **saturated fat** (**hydrogenated oil**). Removing more double bonds makes the saturated fat harder.

$$\text{Unsaturated fat} \ + \ \text{Hydrogen} \ \xrightarrow[\text{catalyst}]{\text{nickel}} \ \text{Saturated fat}$$

Additives

Many processed foods have different substances (**additives**) added to them. This may be to…

- improve the appearance, texture or flavour.
- help preserve the food.

Additives must be shown in the list of ingredients on the label.

Some of the chemical additives that are allowed to be added to foods are called **E-numbers**.

Chemical Analysis

Chemical analysis can be used to identify additives in food. **Chromatography** is used to identify artificial colours, by comparing them to known substances.

1 Samples of five known substances (A, B, C, D and E), and the unknown substance (X) are put on a 'start line' on a piece of paper.

2 The paper is dipped into a solvent. The solvent dissolves the samples and carries them up the paper.

3 Substance X can be identified by comparing the horizontal spots.

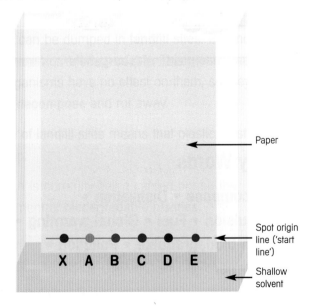

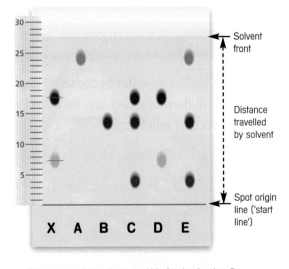

We can see that substance X is food colouring D.

The Earth and Tectonic Theory

Structure of the Earth

The **Earth** is nearly spherical. It has a layered structure that consists of…

- a thin **crust**
- a **mantle**
- a **core** (made of nickel and iron).

Rocks at the Earth's surface are continually being broken up, reformed and changed in an ongoing cycle of events, known as the **rock cycle**. The changes take a very long time.

Crust – 10km–100km thick

Core – has liquid outer part and solid inner part

Mantle – has properties of a solid but flows very slowly

Tectonic Theory

At one time, scientists believed that features on the Earth's surface were caused by shrinkage of the crust when the Earth cooled down, following its formation.

But, as scientists have found out more about the Earth, this **theory** has now been rejected.

Evidence showed scientists that the east coast of South America and the west coast of Africa have…

- **closely matching coastlines**
- **similar patterns of rocks**, which contain **fossils** of the same plants and animals, e.g. the Mesosaurus.

This evidence led Alfred Wegener to propose that South America and Africa had at one time been part of a single land mass. He proposed that the movement of the crust was responsible for the separation of the land, i.e. **continental drift**. This is **tectonic theory**. Unfortunately, Wegener couldn't explain how the crust moved. It took more than 50 years for scientists to discover this.

South America and Africa Now

How South America and Africa Could Have Looked

How the Earth Once Was

Laurasia

Gondwanaland

How the Earth Is Today

Key Words

Additive • Catalyst • Chromatography • Evidence • Fossil • Hydrogenation • Saturated • Theory

The Earth and Tectonic Theory

Tectonic Plates

The Earth's lithosphere (the crust and the upper part of the mantle) is 'cracked' into **tectonic plates**.

Intense heat, released by radioactive decay deep in the Earth, creates convection currents in the mantle which cause the tectonic plates to move apart very slowly, a few centimetres per year.

In convection in a gas or a liquid, the matter rises as it is heated. As it gets further away from the heat source, it cools and sinks. The same happens in the Earth:

1 Hot molten rock rises to the surface, creating new crust.

2 The older, cooler crust, then sinks down where the **convection current** starts to fall.

3 The land masses on these plates move slowly.

The movements are usually small and gradual. But sometimes they can be sudden and disastrous. **Earthquakes** and **volcanic eruptions** are common occurrences at plate boundaries. They are hard to predict.

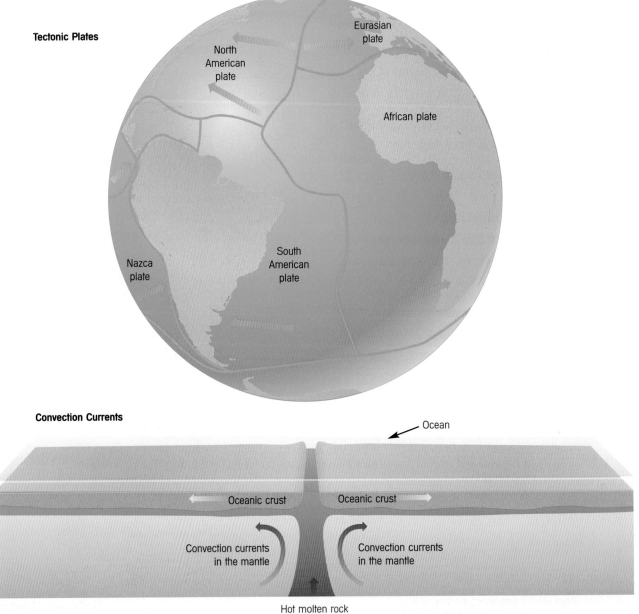

Tectonic Plates

Eurasian plate

North American plate

African plate

Nazca plate

South American plate

Convection Currents

Ocean

Oceanic crust

Oceanic crust

Convection currents in the mantle

Convection currents in the mantle

Hot molten rock

The Earth and Tectonic Theory

Tectonic Plate Movement

Tectonic plates can move in three ways:

1. **Plates slide past each other**, causing huge stresses and strains to build up in the crust. The eventual 'release' of this energy results in an earthquake.
2. **Plates move away from each other** at oceanic ridges, causing fractures to occur. Molten rock rises to the surface, and solidifies to form new ocean floor. These are **constructive plate boundaries**.
3. **Plates move towards each other** in some places when they move away from each other in other places. When they collide, one plate is forced under the other. These are **destructive plate boundaries**.

Sudden plate movement can sometimes have disastrous consequences, for example, **earthquakes**, **volcanoes** and **tsunamis**.

Earthquakes and volcanic eruptions are common on destructive plate boundaries.

Key Words

Tectonic plate • Tsunami

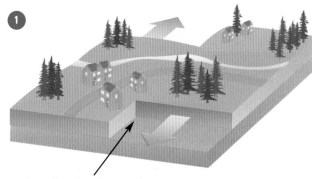

An earthquake will occur along the line where the two plates meet

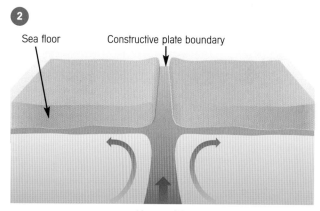

Sea floor — Constructive plate boundary

Magma rising

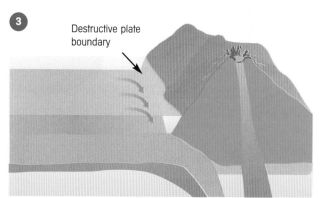

Destructive plate boundary

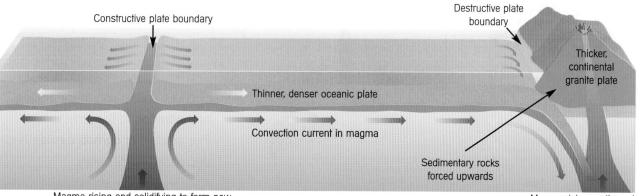

Constructive plate boundary

Thinner, denser oceanic plate

Convection current in magma

Destructive plate boundary

Thicker, continental granite plate

Sedimentary rocks forced upwards

Magma rising and solidifying to form new ocean floor (a few centimetres per year)

Magma rising up through continental crust

The Earth's Atmosphere

The Atmosphere

The **atmosphere** has changed a lot since the formation of the Earth 4.6 billion years ago.

Time Scale	Composition of the Atmosphere	Key Factors and Events which Shaped the Atmosphere

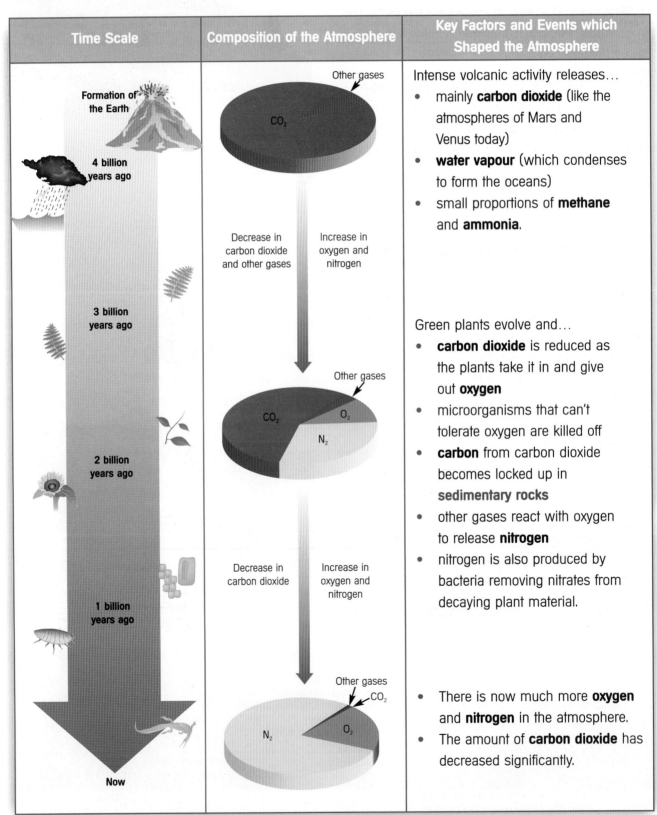

Time Scale:
- Formation of the Earth
- 4 billion years ago
- 3 billion years ago
- 2 billion years ago
- 1 billion years ago
- Now

Composition of the Atmosphere:
- Other gases
- CO₂
- Decrease in carbon dioxide and other gases / Increase in oxygen and nitrogen
- Other gases / CO₂ / O₂ / N₂
- Decrease in carbon dioxide / Increase in oxygen and nitrogen
- Other gases / CO₂ / N₂ / O₂

Key Factors and Events which Shaped the Atmosphere:

Intense volcanic activity releases…
- mainly **carbon dioxide** (like the atmospheres of Mars and Venus today)
- **water vapour** (which condenses to form the oceans)
- small proportions of **methane** and **ammonia**.

Green plants evolve and…
- **carbon dioxide** is reduced as the plants take it in and give out **oxygen**
- microorganisms that can't tolerate oxygen are killed off
- **carbon** from carbon dioxide becomes locked up in **sedimentary rocks**
- other gases react with oxygen to release **nitrogen**
- nitrogen is also produced by bacteria removing nitrates from decaying plant material.

- There is now much more **oxygen** and **nitrogen** in the atmosphere.
- The amount of **carbon dioxide** has decreased significantly.

The Earth's Atmosphere

Composition of the Atmosphere

The proportions of gases in the atmosphere have been more or less the same for about 200 million years. The proportions are shown in the pie chart. **Water vapour** may also be present in varying quantities (0–3%).

The **noble gases** (in Group 0 of the periodic table) are all chemically unreactive gases. They are used in filament lamps and electric discharge tubes. **Helium** is much less dense than air and is used in balloons.

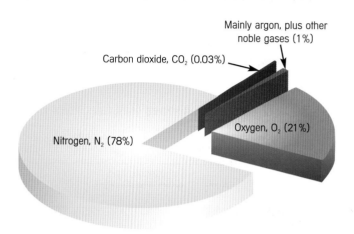

Mainly argon, plus other noble gases (1%)

Carbon dioxide, CO_2 (0.03%)

Nitrogen, N_2 (78%)

Oxygen, O_2 (21%)

Changes to the Atmosphere

The level of carbon dioxide in the atmosphere today is increasing due to…

- **volcanic activity** – geological activity moves carbonate rocks deep into the Earth – during volcanic activity they may release carbon dioxide back into the atmosphere
- **the burning of fossil fuels** – burning carbon, which has been locked up in **fossil fuels** for millions of years, releases carbon dioxide into the atmosphere.

The level of carbon dioxide in the atmosphere is reduced by the reaction between carbon dioxide and sea water. This reaction produces…

- insoluble carbonates which are deposited as sediment
- soluble hydrogencarbonates.

The carbonates form the **sedimentary rocks** in the Earth's crust.

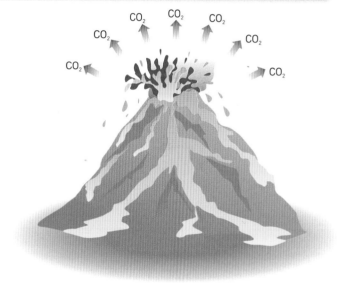

Key Words

Fossil fuel • Sedimentary rock

Unit 1b Summary

Cracking Hydrocarbons

Cracking:

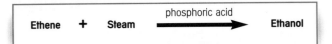

Long-chain hydrocarbon →(heat + catalyst) Short-chain hydrocarbons

Products of cracking = **Alkanes** (saturated hydrocarbons) + **Alkenes** (unsaturated hydrocarbons).

Alkenes = Carbon atoms with double bonds. General formula = C_nH_{2n}

Ethene + Steam →(phosphoric acid) Ethanol

Polymerisation

Polymerisation = Small alkene molecules (monomers) join together to form **polymers**.

Plastics = Synthetic polymers.

General formula for polymerisation:

$$n \left(\begin{array}{c} | \quad | \\ C = C \\ | \quad | \end{array} \right) \longrightarrow \left(\begin{array}{c} | \quad | \\ C - C \\ | \quad | \end{array} \right)_n$$

where n is a very large number

Disposing of Plastics

Burning plastics – produces air pollution, contributes to **global warming**.

Landfill sites – plastics tend to be non-biodegradable so they will not decompose.

Oil

Oil can be extracted from plant materials by **pressing** or by **distillation**.

Vegetable oils provide energy and nutrients, and can be used as a **fuel**. They can be detected using iodine or bromine.

Oils can be used to produce **emulsions**. (Oil + Water = Emulsion)

Hydrogenation

Unsaturated fat heated with hydrogen in presence of nickel catalyst 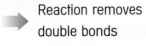 Reaction removes double bonds 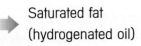 Saturated fat (hydrogenated oil)

Additives

Additives (e.g. E-numbers) are put in food to improve texture, look, flavour, shelf-life.

Chromatography is used to identify artificial colours:

Samples of known substances are put on start line on paper ➡ Paper is dipped in solvent ➡ Solvent dissolves samples, carrying them up paper ➡ Unknown substance is identified

Structure of the Earth

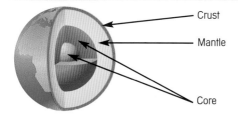

- Crust
- Mantle
- Core

Tectonic Theory

Alfred Wegener proposed that South America and Africa were once a single land mass, due to their closely matching coastlines and similar fossils. Wegener thought crust movement led to the separation of the land.

Tectonic Plates

Earth's lithosphere is 'cracked' into tectonic plates. Convection currents in the mantle cause plates to move.

Tectonic plates can move in three ways:

How Plates Move	Process	Result
Slide past each other	Huge strains build up in crust.	Earthquake
Move away from each other	Fractures occur. Molten rock rises to surface and forms new ocean floor.	Constructive plate boundaries
Move towards each other	Plates collide. One is forced under the other.	Destructive plate boundaries, earthquakes, volcanoes

Earth's Atmosphere

4 billion years ago ➡ 2 billion years ago ➡ Now

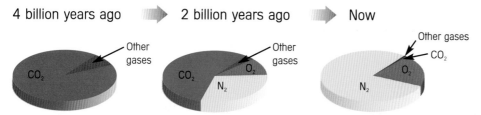

The level of CO_2 in the atmosphere today is increasing due to volcanic activity and the burning of fossil fuels.

Unit 1b Practice Questions

1 Match the words A, B, C and D with the spaces numbered 1 to 4 in the sentences below.

  A alkene   **B** unsaturated

  C cracking   **D** catalyst

The breaking down of larger hydrocarbons to produce smaller, more useful molecules is called ___**1**___.
This is brought about by heating in the presence of a ___**2**___. Certain products of this process contain a
double bond and are said to be ___**3**___. The name given to this type of hydrocarbon is ___**4**___.

2 Match each of the structural formulae A, B, C and D with its correct hydrocarbon name in the list 1 to 4 below.

  A
$$\begin{array}{cc} H & H \\ | & | \\ C = C \\ | & | \\ H & H \end{array}$$

  B
$$\begin{array}{c} H \\ | \\ H - C - H \\ | \\ H \end{array}$$

  C
$$\begin{array}{ccc} H & H & H \\ | & | & | \\ C = C - C - H \\ | & & | \\ H & & H \end{array}$$

  D
$$\begin{array}{cc} H & H \\ | & | \\ H - C - C - H \\ | & | \\ H & H \end{array}$$

  1 Ethane   **2** Ethene   **3** Methane   **4** Propene

3 This question has three parts. For each part, put a tick next to the correct answer.

  a) Polythene (polyethene) is a type of plastic. It is made by joining together lots of small molecules called…

    i) alkanes   **ii)** polymers

    iii) monomers   **iv)** additives

  b) These small molecules belong to a family with the formula…

    i) C_nH_{2n} **ii)** C_nH_{2n+2}

    iii)
$$\left[\begin{array}{cc} | & | \\ C = C \\ | & | \end{array} \right]_n$$

    iv)
$$\left[\begin{array}{cc} | & | \\ C - C \\ | & | \end{array} \right]_n$$

  c) Two useful properties of polythene (polyethene) are that it is…

    i) biodegradable and light   **ii)** cheap and opaque

    iii) biodegradable and waterproof   **iv)** transparent and flexible

4 Suggest two ways in which oils can be extracted from fruit, seeds and nuts.

  a)

  b)

5 a) How is an emulsion made?

_____

b) Give one property of an emulsion.

_____

6 What test can be carried out on a vegetable oil to show that it is unsaturated?

_____

_____

7 Draw and label a diagram and show the three layers of the Earth.

8 a) Give two pieces of evidence which Alfred Wegener used to support his theory that the continents had once been a single land mass.

_____

b) List two ways in which tectonic plates move.

i) _____   **ii)** _____

9 Give the names of two disastrous effects which could happen due to the movement of tectonic plates.

a) _____   **b)** _____

10 The pie charts show the gases in the Earth's early atmosphere and the Earth's atmosphere today.

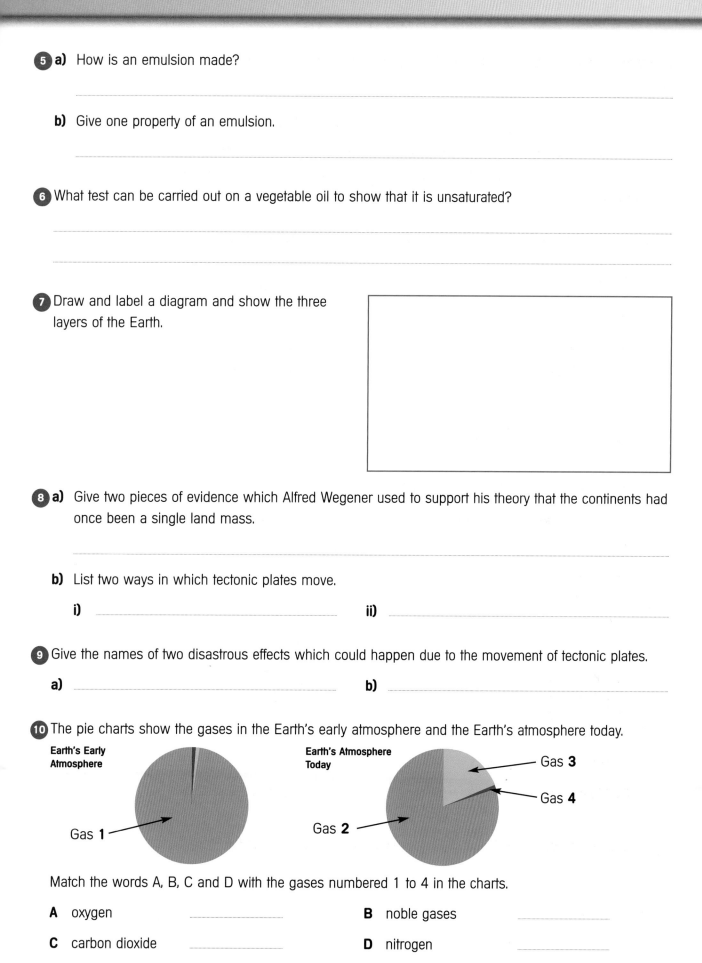

Earth's Early Atmosphere

Gas **1**

Earth's Atmosphere Today

Gas **3**

Gas **4**

Gas **2**

Match the words A, B, C and D with the gases numbered 1 to 4 in the charts.

A oxygen _____   **B** noble gases _____

C carbon dioxide _____   **D** nitrogen _____

Atoms

Atoms

Atoms have a small central nucleus which is made up of **protons** and **neutrons**. The **nucleus** is surrounded by **electrons**.

Protons, neutrons and electrons have relative **electrical charges**.

Atomic Particle	Relative Charge
Proton	+1
Neutron	0
Electron	-1

Atoms as a whole have **no overall charge** as they contain an **equal number** of **protons** and **electrons**.

All atoms of a particular element have the **same number of protons**. Atoms of different elements have **different numbers** of **protons**. The number of protons in an atom is called its **atomic number**.

Elements are arranged in the modern periodic table in order of **atomic number**.

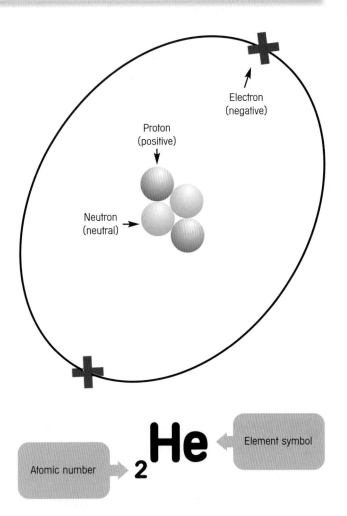

Electron (negative)

Proton (positive)

Neutron (neutral)

Atomic number $\rightarrow$ $_2$**He** $\leftarrow$ Element symbol

Electron Configuration and Structure

Electrons in an atom occupy the lowest available **energy level** (i.e. the innermost available shell).

- The **first** level can only contain a **maximum of 2 electrons**.
- The energy levels after this can each hold a **maximum of 8 electrons**.

The **electron configuration** tells us how the electrons are arranged around the nucleus in **energy levels** or **shells**. It is written as a series of numbers, for example…

- oxygen is 2,6
- aluminium is 2,8,3

The **periodic table** groups together the elements in terms of **electronic structure**.

Elements in the **same group** have the same number of **electrons** in their **highest energy level (outer shell)**. They also have **similar properties**.

A particular energy level is gradually filled with electrons from **left to right**, across each **period**.

Key Words

Atomic number • Compound • Covalent bond • Electron • Ionic bond • Neutron • Nucleus • Proton

Alkali Metals and Halogens

The Alkali Metals (Group 1)

The alkali metals…
- have 1 electron in their outermost shell
- react with **non-metal elements** to form **ionic compounds** where the metal ion has a single **positive** charge.

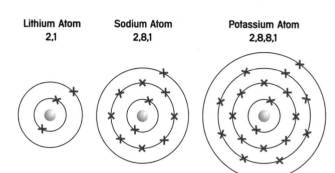

Lithium Atom 2,1 Sodium Atom 2,8,1 Potassium Atom 2,8,8,1

The Halogens (Group 7)

The halogens…
- have 7 electrons in their outermost shell
- react with **alkali metals** to form **ionic compounds** where the halide ions have a single **negative** charge.

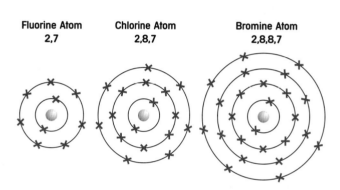

Fluorine Atom 2,7 Chlorine Atom 2,8,7 Bromine Atom 2,8,8,7

Mixtures and Compounds

A **mixture** consists of two or more elements or **compounds** that are **not chemically combined**. The properties of the substances remain unchanged and specific to that substance.

Compounds are substances in which the atoms of two or more elements **are chemically combined** (not just mixed together).

Atoms can form chemical bonds by…
- **sharing electrons** (covalent bonds)
- **gaining** or **losing electrons** (ionic bonds).

When atoms form **chemical bonds**, the arrangement of the **outer shell** of electrons **changes**. This results in each atom getting a **complete outer shell** of electrons. For most atoms this is eight electrons, but for helium it is only two.

HT Simple Molecular Compounds

Substances that consist of **simple molecules** are gases, liquids and solids that have relatively **low melting** and **boiling points**. This is because they only have weak intermolecular forces (forces between their molecules). The molecules have no overall electrical charge, so they can't conduct electricity.

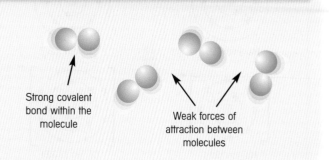

Strong covalent bond within the molecule

Weak forces of attraction between molecules

Ionic Bonding

Ionic Compounds

Ionic compounds are giant structures of **ions**. They are held together by **strong forces** of attraction (electrostatic forces) between **oppositely charged ions**, that act in **all directions**. This type of bonding is called **ionic bonding**.

Ionic compounds…

- have **high melting** and **boiling points**
- **conduct electricity** when molten or in solution because the charged ions are free to move about and carry the current.

(+) Positively charged ion   (–) Negatively charged ion

The Ionic Bond

An **ionic bond** occurs between a **metal** and a **non-metal** atom. It involves a **transfer** of **electrons** from one atom to the other.

This forms electrically charged **ions**, each of which has a complete outer energy level.

They have the electronic structure of a noble gas.

- Atoms which **lose electrons** become **positively** charged ions.
- Atoms which **gain electrons** become **negatively** charged ions.

Example 1
Sodium (Na) and chlorine (Cl) bond ionically to form sodium chloride, NaCl.

1. The sodium atom has 1 electron in its outer shell.
2. The electron is transferred to the chlorine atom.
3. Both atoms now have 8 electrons in their outer shell.
4. The atoms become ions, Na^+ and Cl^-.
5. The compound formed is sodium chloride, NaCl.

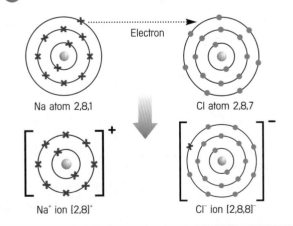

Na atom 2,8,1   Cl atom 2,8,7

Na^+ ion $[2,8]^+$ Cl^- ion $[2,8,8]^-$

Example 2
Magnesium (Mg) and oxygen (O) bond ionically to form magnesium oxide, MgO.

1. The magnesium atom has 2 electrons in its outer shell.
2. These 2 electrons are transferred to the oxygen atom.
3. Both atoms now have 8 electrons in their outer shell.
4. The atoms become ions, Mg^{2+} and O^{2-}.
5. The compound formed is magnesium oxide, MgO.

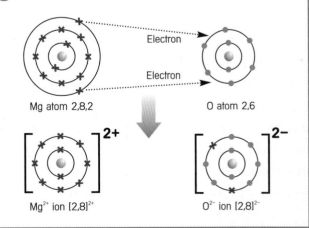

Mg atom 2,8,2   O atom 2,6

Mg^{2+} ion $[2,8]^{2+}$ O^{2-} ion $[2,8]^{2-}$

Covalent Bonding

The Covalent Bond

A **covalent bond** occurs between **non-metal atoms**. It is a strong bond which is formed when **pairs of electrons are shared**.

Some covalently bonded substances have **simple bonds**, e.g. H_2, Cl_2, O_2, HCl, H_2O and CH_4.

Others have **giant covalent structures**, called **macromolecules**, e.g. diamond and silicon dioxide.

Atoms which share electrons usually have **low melting** and **boiling points**. This is because they often form molecules in which there are...

- **strong covalent bonds** between the **atoms**
- **weak forces of attraction** between the **molecules**.

Key Words

Covalent bond • Electron • Ion • Ionic bond

Example

1. A chlorine atom has 7 electrons in its outer shell.
2. In order to bond with another chlorine atom, an electron from each atom is shared.
3. This gives each chlorine atom 8 electrons in the outer shell.
4. Each atom now has a complete outer shell.

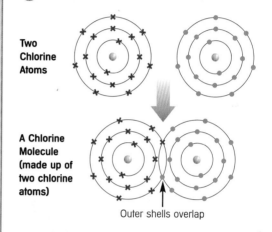

Two Chlorine Atoms

A Chlorine Molecule (made up of two chlorine atoms)

Outer shells overlap

Covalent Bonding

There are three different methods for representing the covalent bonds in each molecule. You need to be familiar with the following examples, and know how to use the different methods.

The two most common forms are shown in this table:

The third form is shown here for an ammonia molecule. But, unless specifically asked for, you should use the other two methods.

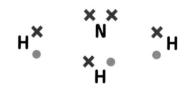

Molecule	Water H_2O	Chlorine Cl_2	Hydrogen H_2	Hydrogen chloride, HCl	Methane CH_4	Oxygen O_2
Method 1	H O H	Cl Cl	H H	H Cl	H C H (with H above and below)	O O
Method 2	H–O–H	Cl–Cl	H–H	H–Cl	H–C–H (with H above and below)	O=O (a double bond)

Covalent Structures

Giant Covalent Structures

All the atoms in giant covalent structures are linked by **strong covalent bonds**. This means they have very **high melting points**.

Diamond is a form of carbon that has a **giant, rigid covalent structure** (lattice). Each carbon atom forms **four covalent bonds** with other carbon atoms.

Diamond has a **large number of covalent bonds** so it is a very **hard substance**.

Graphite is a form of carbon that also has a giant covalent structure. However, in graphite, each carbon atom forms **three covalent bonds** with other carbon atoms in a layered structure.

Graphite has layers that can slide past each other, making it soft and slippery.

(HT) In graphite, one electron from each carbon atom is delocalised. These delocalised electrons allow graphite to **conduct heat and electricity**.

Silicon dioxide (or silica, SiO_2) has a lattice structure similar to diamond. Each **oxygen** atom is joined to **two silicon atoms**, and each **silicon** atom is joined to **four oxygen atoms**.

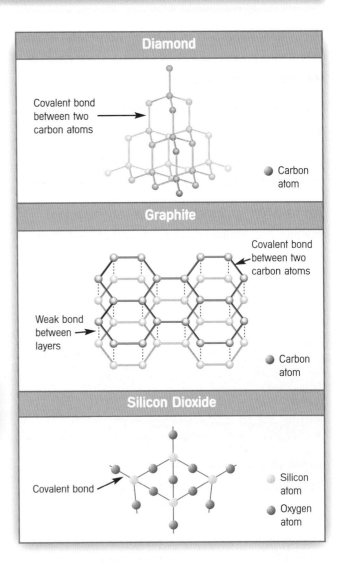

Diamond

Covalent bond between two carbon atoms

Carbon atom

Graphite

Covalent bond between two carbon atoms

Weak bond between layers

Carbon atom

Silicon Dioxide

Covalent bond

Silicon atom

Oxygen atom

Metals

The layers of atoms in metals are able to slide over each other. This means that metals can be **bent and shaped**.

(HT) Metals have a giant structure in which electrons in the highest energy level can be **delocalised**.

This produces a regular arrangement (lattice) of **positive ions** that are held together by electrons using electrostatic attraction.

These delocalised electrons can move around freely. This allows metal to **conduct heat and electricity**.

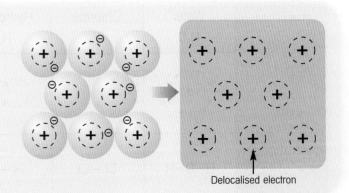

Delocalised electron

Nanoparticles and Nanostructures

Nanoscience is the study of very small structures. The structures are 1–100 nanometres in size, roughly in the order of a few hundred atoms.

One **nanometre** is 0.000 000 001 m (one billionth of a metre) and is written as 1 nm or 1 m x 10^{-9}.

Nanoparticles are tiny, tiny particles that can combine to form structures called **nanostructures**.

Nanostructures can be manipulated so materials can be developed that have new and specific properties.

The **properties** of **nanoparticles** are different to the properties of the **same materials in bulk**.

For example…
- electrons can move through an insulating layer of atoms
- nanoparticles are more sensitive to light, heat and magnetism
- nanoparticles have a high surface area in relation to their volume.

Human Hair	Virus / Small Bacteria	Atoms and Small Molecules
0.000 01 metre = 1 x 10^{-5}m	0.000 000 1 metre = 1 x 10^{-7}m	0.000 000 001 metre = 1 x 10^{-9}m
Can be seen using a microscope	Can be seen using an electron microscope	Nanoparticle zone

Nanocomposites

Other materials can be added to plastics to make **nanocomposite** materials. In comparison to plastics, nanocomposites can be…
- stronger
- stiffer
- lighter.

The characteristics of nanocomposites can be seen by looking at the nanostructures formed by the nanoparticles.

Nanocomposites are already being used or developed for many industries, for example…
- the car industry
- medical and dental applications
- new computers
- highly selective sensors
- new coatings and sunscreens
- stronger and lighter construction materials
- product-specific catalysts.

Smart materials are a type of nanostructure that can be designed to…
- have specific properties on a nanoscopic scale
- behave in a certain way when subjected to certain conditions.

Key Words

Covalent bond • Nanoscience • Smart material

The Periodic Table and Atoms

The Periodic Table

1	2											3	4	5	6	7	8 or 0
						1 **H** hydrogen 1											**4** **He** helium 2
7 **Li** lithium 3	**9** **Be** beryllium 4											**11** **B** boron 5	**12** **C** carbon 6	**14** **N** nitrogen 7	**16** **O** oxygen 8	**19** **F** fluorine 9	**20** **Ne** neon 10
23 **Na** sodium 11	**24** **Mg** magnesium 12											**27** **Al** aluminium 13	**28** **Si** silicon 14	**31** **P** phosphorus 15	**32** **S** sulfur 16	**35.5** **Cl** chlorine 17	**40** **Ar** argon 18
39 **K** potassium 19	**40** **Ca** calcium 20	**45** **Sc** scandium 21	**48** **Ti** titanium 22	**51** **V** vanadium 23	**52** **Cr** chromium 24	**55** **Mn** manganese 25	**56** **Fe** iron 26	**59** **Co** cobalt 27	**59** **Ni** nickel 28	**63.5** **Cu** copper 29	**65** **Zn** zinc 30	**70** **Ga** gallium 31	**73** **Ge** germanium 32	**75** **As** arsenic 33	**79** **Se** selenium 34	**80** **Br** bromine 35	**84** **Kr** krypton 36
85 **Rb** rubidium 37	**88** **Sr** strontium 38	**89** **Y** yttrium 39	**91** **Zr** zirconium 40	**93** **Nb** niobium 41	**96** **Mo** molybdenum 42	**[98]** **Tc** technetium 43	**101** **Ru** ruthenium 44	**103** **Rh** rhodium 45	**106** **Pd** palladium 46	**108** **Ag** silver 47	**112** **Cd** cadmium 48	**115** **In** indium 49	**119** **Sn** tin 50	**122** **Sb** antimony 51	**128** **Te** tellurium 52	**127** **I** iodine 53	**131** **Xe** xenon 54
133 **Cs** caesium 55	**137** **Ba** barium 56	**139** **La*** lanthanum 57	**178** **Hf** hafnium 72	**181** **Ta** tantalum 73	**184** **W** tungsten 74	**186** **Re** rhenium 75	**190** **Os** osmium 76	**192** **Ir** iridium 77	**195** **Pt** platinum 78	**197** **Au** gold 79	**201** **Hg** mercury 80	**204** **Tl** thallium 81	**207** **Pb** lead 82	**209** **Bi** bismuth 83	**[209]** **Po** polonium 84	**[210]** **At** astatine 85	**[222]** **Rn** radon 86
[223] **Fr** francium 87	**[226]** **Ra** radium 88	**[227]** **Ac*** actinium 89	**[261]** **Rf** rutherfordium 104	**[262]** **Db** dubnium 105	**[266]** **Sg** seaborgium 106	**[264]** **Bh** bohrium 107	**[277]** **Hs** hassium 108	**[268]** **Mt** meitnerium 109	**[271]** **Ds** darmstadtium 110	**[272]** **Rg** roentgenium 111							

N.B. The exact position of mass number, element name and atomic number may differ depending on the version of periodic table. However, the mass number will always be the top number, and the atomic number the bottom number.

Mass Number and Atomic Number

Atoms of an element can be described using their mass and atomic number.

The **mass number** is the total number of **protons** and **neutrons** in the atom.

The **atomic (proton) number** is the number of protons in the atom.

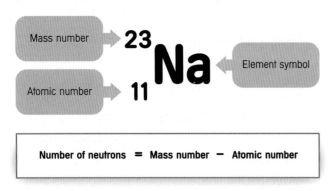

Mass number → ^{23}**Na** ← Element symbol

Atomic number → $_{11}$

Number of neutrons = Mass number − Atomic number

The number of **protons** in an atom is **equal** to the number of **electrons**. So, an atom has **no overall charge**.

1 Hydrogen

$^{1}_{1}$**H**

1 proton
1 electron

2 Oxygen

$^{16}_{8}$**O**

8 protons
8 electrons

Although they have the same charge, protons and electrons have a **different mass**.

Atomic Particle	Relative Mass
Proton ●	1
Neutron ●	1
Electron ✖	Very small (negligible)

Isotopes and Relative Formula Mass

Isotopes

All atoms of a **particular element** have the **same number** of protons. Atoms of **different elements** have **different numbers** of protons.

Isotopes are atoms of the **same element** which have **different numbers of neutrons**.

Isotopes have the **same atomic number** but a **different mass number**.

For example, chlorine has two isotopes:

1 **Chlorine**

$$_{17}^{35}\text{Cl}$$

17 protons
17 electrons
18 neutrons (35 − 17)

2 **Chlorine**

$$_{17}^{37}\text{Cl}$$

17 protons
17 electrons
20 neutrons (37 − 17)

HT Relative Atomic Mass, A_r

The relative atomic mass, A_r is the mass of a particular atom compared with a twelfth of the mass of a carbon atom (the ^{12}C isotope).

The A_r is an **average** value for all the **isotopes** of the element.

The **mass number** of the element is the same as the A_r of the element.

By looking at the periodic table, you can see that...
- carbon is 12 times heavier than hydrogen, but is only half as heavy as magnesium
- magnesium is three quarters as heavy as sulfur
- sulfur is twice as heavy as oxygen, etc.

You can use this idea to calculate the relative formula mass of compounds.

Relative Formula Mass, M_r

The relative formula mass, M_r, of a compound is the relative atomic masses of all its elements added together.

To calculate M_r, you need to know...
- the formula of the compound
- the A_r of all the atoms involved.

Example 1
Calculate the M_r of water, H_2O.

Write the formula ▶ $$H_2O$$

Substitute the A_rs ▶ (2 x 1) + 16

Calculate the M_r ▶ 2 + 16 = 18

Key Words

Atomic number • Electron • Isotope • Mass number • Neutron • Proton • Relative atomic mass **• Relative formula mass**

Example 2
Calculate the M_r of potassium carbonate, K_2CO_3.

Write the formula ▶ $$K_2CO_3$$

Substitute the A_rs ▶ (39 x 2) + 12 + (16 x 3)

Calculate the M_r ▶ 78 + 12 + 48 = 138

Percentage Mass

Calculating Percentage Mass

The mass of the compound is its **relative formula mass**.

To calculate the **percentage mass** of an element in a compound, you need to know…
- the **formula** of the compound
- the **relative atomic mass** of all the atoms.

You can calculate the percentage mass by using this formula…

$$\frac{\text{Relative mass of element in the compound}}{\text{Relative formula mass of compound } (M_r)} \quad \text{X} \quad 100$$

Example 1

Calculate the percentage mass of magnesium in magnesium oxide, MgO.

Relative mass of magnesium = 24
Relative formula mass (M_r) of MgO =
$$24 + 16 = 40$$

A_r Mg A_r O A_r MgO

$$\frac{\text{Relative mass of element}}{M_r \text{ of compound}} \times 100$$

$$= \frac{24}{40} \times 100 = \textbf{60\%}$$

Example 2

Calculate the percentage mass of potassium in potassium carbonate, K_2CO_3.

Relative mass of potassium = 39 x 2
Relative formula mass (M_r) of K_2CO_3 =
$$78 + 12 + 48 = 138$$

A_r K x 2 A_r C A_r O x 3 A_r K_2CO_3

$$\frac{\text{Relative mass of element}}{M_r \text{ of compound}} \times 100$$

$$= \frac{78}{138} \times 100 = \textbf{56.5\%}$$

(HT) Empirical Formula of a Compound

The empirical formula of a compound is the **simplest formula** that represents the **composition** of the compound **by mass**.

Example

Find the simplest formula of an oxide of iron produced by reacting 1.12g of iron with 0.48g of oxygen (A_r Fe = 56, A_r O = 16).

Identify the mass of the elements in the compound

Masses: Fe = 1.12, O = 0.48

Divide these masses by their relative atomic masses

$$\text{Fe} = \frac{1.12}{56} = 0.02 \qquad \text{O} = \frac{0.48}{16} = 0.03$$

Identify the ratio of atoms in the compound

Ratio =   0.02 : 0.03

x 100   x 100
                2 : 3

Empirical formula = $\textbf{Fe}_2\textbf{O}_3$

The Mole

A **mole** (mol) is a measure of the **number of particles** (atoms or molecules) contained in a substance.

One mole of **any substance** (element or compound) will always contain the **same number** of particles – six hundred thousand billion billion or 6×10^{23}. This is the **relative formula mass** of the substance.

If a substance is an **element**, the mass of one mole of the substance, called the molar mass (g/mol), is always **equal** to the **relative atomic mass** of the substance in grams. For example…

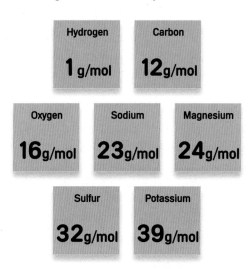

Hydrogen	Carbon
1 g/mol	**12** g/mol

Oxygen	Sodium	Magnesium
16 g/mol	**23** g/mol	**24** g/mol

Sulfur	Potassium
32 g/mol	**39** g/mol

If a substance is a **compound**, the mass of one mole of the substance is always **equal** to the **relative formula mass** of the substance in grams. For example, one mole of sodium hydroxide (NaOH)…

A_r sodium + A_r hydrogen + A_r oxygen

= 23 + 1 + 16 = **40g**

You can calculate the number of moles in a substance using this formula:

$$\text{Number of moles of substance (mol)} = \frac{\text{Mass of substance (g)}}{\text{Mass of one mole (g/mol)}}$$

N.B. You need to remember this equation as it will not be given to you in the exam.

Example 1

Calculate the number of moles of carbon in 36g of the element.

$$\text{Number of moles of substance (mol)} = \frac{\text{Mass of substance (g)}}{\text{Mass of one mole (g/mol)}}$$

$$= \frac{36g}{12g/mol} \quad A_r \text{ carbon} = 12$$

= **3 moles**

Example 2

Calculate the number of moles of carbon dioxide in 33g of the gas.

$$\text{Number of moles of substance (mol)} = \frac{\text{Mass of substance (g)}}{\text{Mass of one mole (g/mol)}}$$

$$= \frac{33g}{44g/mol}$$

A_r carbon dioxide = A_r carbon + 2 × A_r oxygen = 12 + (2 × 16) = 44

= **0.75 mole**

Example 3

Calculate the mass of 4 moles of sodium hydroxide.

Rearrange the formula…

$$\text{Mass of substance (g)} = \text{Number of moles of substance (mol)} \times \text{Mass of one mole (g/mol)}$$

= 4mol × 40g/mol

= **160g**

N.B. If you are confident in your mathematical ability, you can also do these calculations using ratios.

Key Words

Mole • Relative atomic mass • Relative formula mass

Calculating Mass

HT Calculating the Mass of a Product

Example

Calculate how much calcium oxide can be produced from 50kg of calcium carbonate.
(Relative atomic masses: Ca = 40, C = 12, O = 16).

1. Write down the equation.
2. Work out the M_r of each substance.
3. Check that the total mass of reactants equals the total mass of the products. If they are not the same, check your work.
4. The question only mentions calcium oxide and calcium carbonate, so you can now ignore the carbon dioxide. You just need the ratio of mass of reactant to mass of product.
5. Use the ratio to calculate how much calcium oxide can be produced.

1

$$CaCO_3 \longrightarrow CaO + CO_2$$

2

$$40 + 12 + (3 \times 16) \longrightarrow (40 + 16) + [12 + (2 \times 16)]$$

3

$$100 \longrightarrow 56 + 44 \checkmark$$

4

$$100 : 56$$

5

If 100kg of $CaCO_3$ produces 56kg of CaO, then 1kg of $CaCO_3$ produces $\frac{56}{100}$ kg of CaO, and 50kg of $CaCO_3$ produces $\frac{56}{100} \times 50$
= 28kg of CaO.

HT Calculating the Mass of a Reactant

Example

Calculate how much aluminium oxide is needed to produce 540 tonnes of aluminium.
(Relative atomic masses: Al = 27, O = 16).

1. Write down the equation.
2. Work out the M_r of each substance.
3. Check that the total mass of reactants equals the total mass of the products. If they are not the same, check your work.
4. The question only mentions aluminium oxide and aluminium, so you can now ignore the oxygen. You just need the ratio of mass of reactant to mass of product.
5. Use the ratio to calculate how much aluminium oxide is needed.

1

$$2Al_2O_3 \longrightarrow 4Al + 3O_2$$

2

$$2 \times [(2 \times 27) + (3 \times 16)] \longrightarrow (4 \times 27) + [3 \times (2 \times 16)]$$

3

$$204 \longrightarrow 108 + 96 \checkmark$$

4

$$204 : 108$$

5

If 204 tonnes of Al_2O_3 produces 108 tonnes of Al, then $\frac{204}{108}$ tonnes is needed to produce 1 tonne of Al, and $\frac{204}{108} \times 540$ tonnes is needed to produce 540 tonnes of Al
= 1020 tonnes of Al_2O_3.

Yield and Atom Economy

Yield

Atoms are **never lost or gained** in a chemical reaction. But, it isn't always possible to obtain the calculated amount of the product because…

- if the reaction is reversible, it might not go to completion
- some product could be lost when it is separated from the reaction mixture
- some of the reactants may react in different ways to the expected reaction.

HT The amount of product obtained is called the yield.

The **percentage yield** can be calculated by comparing…
- the actual yield obtained from a reaction
- the maximum theoretical yield.

$$\text{Percentage yield} = \frac{\text{Yield from reaction}}{\text{Maximum theoretical yield}} \times 100$$

Example

50kg of calcium carbonate ($CaCO_3$) is expected to produce 28kg of calcium oxide (CaO).

A company heats 50kg of calcium carbonate in a kiln and obtains 22kg of calcium oxide.

Calculate the percentage yield.

$$\text{Percentage yield} = \frac{22}{28} \times 100 = \textbf{78.6\%}$$

Calculating Atom Economy

Chemical reactions often produce more than one **product**. However, not all of these products are **'useful'**. A useful product is one that can be used in industry.

Atom economy (atom utilisation) is a measure of the **amount of starting materials** (reactants) that end up as **useful products**.

$$\text{Atom economy} = \frac{M_r \text{ of useful products}}{M_r \text{ of reactants}} \times 100$$

In industry, it's important to use reactions which have a **high atom economy** in order to…
- make the reaction economical
- ensure sustainable development.

Example

Calcium carbonate → Calcium oxide + Carbon dioxide

The products of this reaction are calcium oxide (useful) and carbon dioxide (waste).

Calculate the atom economy of this reaction.

1 Calculate the M_r of the reactants and products

$$CaCO_3 \longrightarrow CaCO + CO_2$$

M_r of $CaCO_3$ = 40 + 12 + (3 x 16) = **100**

M_r of CaCO = 40 + 16 = **56**

M_r of CO_2 = 12 + (2 x 16) = **44**

2 Calculate the atom economy

$$\text{Atom economy} = \frac{56}{100} \times 100$$
$$= \textbf{56\%}$$

Key Words

Atom economy • Yield

Reversible Reactions & the Haber Process

Reversible Reactions

Some chemical reactions are **reversible**. In a **reversible reaction**, the **products** can **react** to produce the **original reactants**.

These reactions are represented as…

$$A \; + \; B \; \rightleftharpoons \; C \; + \; D$$

This means that A and B can react to produce C and D, and C and D can also react to produce A and B.

For example…

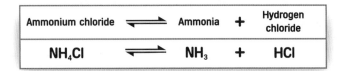

Ammonium chloride $\rightleftharpoons$	Ammonia	+	Hydrogen chloride
NH_4Cl $\rightleftharpoons$	NH_3	+	HCl

Solid ammonium chloride decomposes when heated to produce ammonia and hydrogen chloride gas (both colourless).

Ammonia reacts with hydrogen chloride gas to produce clouds of white ammonium chloride powder.

The Haber Process

Reversible reactions may not go to completion. However, they can still be used efficiently in continuous processes such as the **Haber Process.**

The Haber process is used to manufacture **ammonia**. The raw materials for this process are…
- **nitrogen** – from the fractional distillation of liquid air
- **hydrogen** – from natural gas and steam.

The purified nitrogen and hydrogen are passed over an **iron catalyst** at a…
- **high temperature** (about 450°C)
- **high pressure** (about 200 atmospheres).

Some of the hydrogen and nitrogen **reacts** to **form ammonia**.

The **ammonia** produced can **break down** again into **nitrogen** and **hydrogen**.

Nitrogen	+	Hydrogen $\rightleftharpoons$	Ammonia
N_2	+	$3H_2$ $\rightleftharpoons$	$2NH_3$

HT These reaction conditions are chosen to produce a **reasonable** yield of ammonia quickly.

Even so, only **some** of the hydrogen and nitrogen react together to form ammonia.

The Haber Process

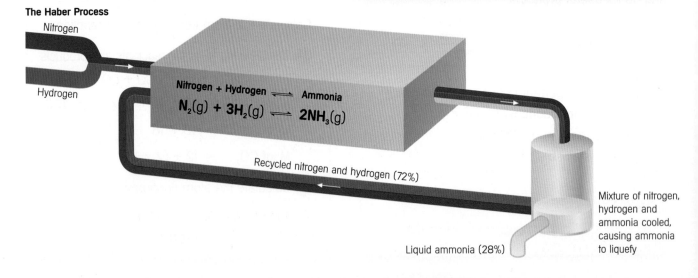

Nitrogen

Hydrogen

Nitrogen + Hydrogen $\rightleftharpoons$ Ammonia
$N_2(g) + 3H_2(g) \rightleftharpoons 2NH_3(g)$

Recycled nitrogen and hydrogen (72%)

Liquid ammonia (28%)

Mixture of nitrogen, hydrogen and ammonia cooled, causing ammonia to liquefy

Chemical Reactions

Rates of Reactions

Chemical reactions only occur when reacting particles **collide** with each other with **sufficient energy**.

The **minimum amount** of energy required to cause a reaction is called the **activation energy**.

There are four important factors which affect the rate of reaction:

- Temperature.
- Concentration.
- Surface area.
- Use of a catalyst.

Temperature

In a **cold** reaction mixture, the particles move quite **slowly**. They collide less often, with less energy, so **fewer collisions** are successful.

In a **hot** reaction mixture the particles move more **quickly**. They collide more often, with greater energy, so **more collisions** are successful.

Cold Reaction	Hot Reaction

Concentration

In a **low concentration** reaction, the particles are **spread out**. They collide less often, so there are fewer successful collisions.

In a **high concentration** reaction, the particles are crowded **close together**. They collide more often, so there are more successful collisions.

Increasing the **pressure** of reacting gases also increases the frequency of collisions.

Low Concentration	High Concentration

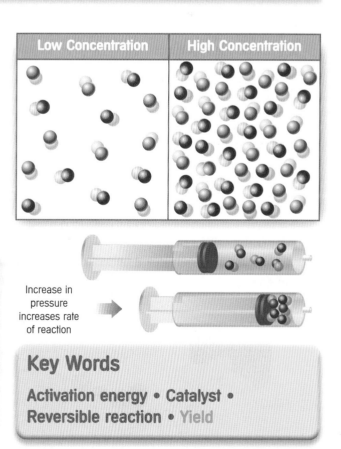

Increase in pressure increases rate of reaction

HT **Concentrations** of solutions are given in **moles per cubic decimetre (mol/dm^3)**.

Equal volumes of solutions of the same molar concentration contain the same number of moles of solute, i.e. the same number of particles.

Equal volumes of gases at the same temperature and pressure contain the **same number** of molecules.

Key Words

Activation energy • Catalyst • Reversible reaction • Yield

Chemical Reactions

Surface Area

Large pieces of a solid reactant have a **small surface area** in relation to their volume.

Fewer particles are exposed and available for collisions. This means **fewer collisions** and a **slower reaction**.

Small pieces of a solid reactant have a **large surface area** in relation to their volume, so more particles are exposed and available for collisions.

This means **more collisions** and a **faster reaction**.

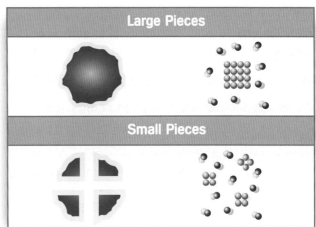

Large Pieces

Small Pieces

Using a Catalyst

A **catalyst** is a substance which **increases the rate** of a chemical reaction without being used up or altered in the process.

A catalyst...
- reduces the amount of energy needed for a successful collision
- makes more collisions successful
- speeds up the reaction
- provides a surface for the molecules to attach to, which increases their chances of bumping into each other.

Different reactions need different catalysts, e.g....
- the cracking of hydrocarbons uses broken pottery
- the manufacture of ammonia uses iron.

Increasing the rates of chemical reactions is important in industry because it helps to **reduce costs**.

Catalyst Provides Larger Surface Area

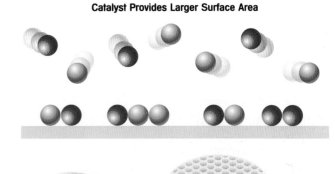

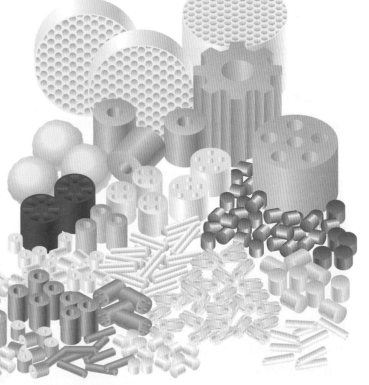

Analysing the Rate of Reaction

$$\text{Rate of Reaction} = \frac{\text{Amount of reactant used / product formed}}{\text{Time}}$$

The rate of a chemical reaction can be found by:

1 Measuring the amount of reactants used.
If one of the products is a gas, you could weigh the reaction mixture before and after the reaction takes place. The mass of the mixture will decrease.

2 Measuring the amount of products formed.
You could use a gas syringe to measure the total volume of gas produced at timed intervals.

Plotting Reaction Rates

Graphs can be plotted to show the progress of a chemical reaction. There are three things to remember:

1 The steeper the line, the faster the reaction.
2 When one of the reactants is used up, the reaction stops (lines become horizontal).
3 The same amount of product is formed from the same amount of reactants, irrespective of rate.

The graph shows us that reaction **A** is faster than reaction **B**. This could be because...

- the surface area of the solid reactants in **A** is greater than in **B**
- the temperature of reaction **A** is greater than reaction **B**
- the concentration of the solution in **A** is greater than in **B**
- a catalyst is used in reaction **A** but not in reaction **B**.

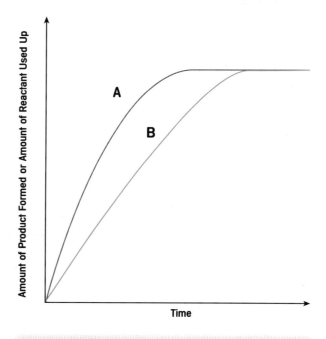

Key Word

Catalyst

Exothermic and Endothermic Reactions

Chemical Reactions

When chemical reactions occur, **energy** is transferred **to** or **from** the **surroundings**.

Many chemical reactions are, therefore, accompanied by a **temperature change**.

Exothermic Reactions

Exothermic reactions are accompanied by a **temperature rise**. They transfer heat energy to the surroundings, i.e. they **give out** heat.

Common examples of exothermic reactions include…

- neutralising alkalis with acids
- oxidation
- combustion.

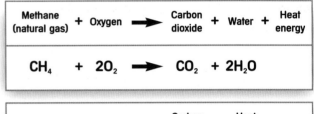

$$CH_4 + 2O_2 \longrightarrow CO_2 + 2H_2O$$

$$C + O_2 \longrightarrow CO_2$$

Endothermic Reactions

Endothermic reactions are accompanied by a **fall in temperature**. Heat energy is transferred from the surroundings, i.e. they **take in** heat.

Thermal decomposition and dissolving ammonium nitrate crystals in water are examples of endothermic reactions.

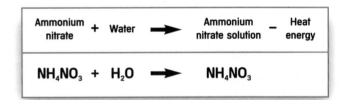

$$NH_4NO_3 + H_2O \longrightarrow NH_4NO_3$$

(HT) Changing Reaction Conditions

In an **exothermic** reaction…
- if the temperature is **raised**, the yield **decreases**
- if the temperature is **lowered**, the yield **increases**.

In an **endothermic** reaction…
- if the temperature is **raised**, the yield **increases**
- if the temperature is **lowered**, the yield **decreases**.

In **gaseous reactions,** an increase in pressure favours the reaction which produces the least number of molecules.

These factors, together with reaction rates, determine the optimum conditions in industrial processes, e.g. the **Haber process**.

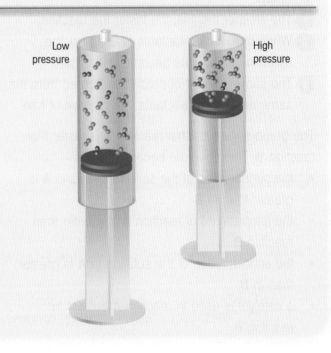

Low pressure

High pressure

Reversible Reactions

If a **reversible reaction** is **exothermic in one direction**, then it follows that it is **endothermic in the opposite direction**. The **same amount of energy** is transferred in each case.

An example of this is when hydrated copper sulfate is gently heated.

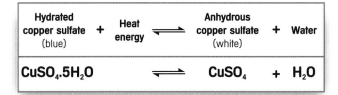

Hydrated copper sulfate (blue)	+	Heat energy	$\rightleftharpoons$	Anhydrous copper sulfate (white)	+	Water
$CuSO_4.5H_2O$			$\rightleftharpoons$	$CuSO_4$	+	H_2O

If water is added to white anhydrous copper sulfate, heat is given out and blue hydrated copper sulfate is formed.

The blue crystals of hydrated copper sulfate can then be heated. Heat is taken in, the water is removed, and white anhydrous copper sulfate is formed.

This reverse reaction can be used as a test for the presence of water. If the copper sulfate changes from white to blue then water is present.

Hydrated Copper Sulfate

Anhydrous Copper Sulfate

Water Being Added to Anhydrous Copper Sulfate

Sustainable Development

It is important to minimise energy use and wastage in industrial processes for…
* sustainable development
* economic reasons.

Non-vigorous conditions mean…
* less energy is used
* less energy is released into the environment
* a less efficient reaction.

In an **industrial process production**…
* an **efficient** reaction takes place in a short time, so less energy is needed or wasted, and the cost is reduced
* an **inefficient** reaction takes a long time, so more energy is needed and wasted, so more energy is used.

Key Words

Endothermic • Exothermic • Reversible reaction • Yield

Reversible Reactions & Closed Systems

HT Reversible Reactions

The manufacture of ammonia in the **Haber process** is a **reversible reaction**. It involves energy transfers associated with the **breaking** and **forming** of chemical bonds.

$$N_2 \ + \ 3H_2 \ \underset{\text{Endothermic}}{\overset{\text{Exothermic}}{\rightleftharpoons}} \ 2NH_3$$

The **volume** of ammonia produced is **less** than the total volume of the **reactants** (nitrogen and hydrogen).

Less energy is needed to **break the bonds** between the nitrogen and hydrogen molecules than is **released** in the **formation** of the ammonia molecules.

Altering the **temperature** and **pressure** can have a big impact on the production of ammonia:

- **High pressure** produces a high yield at a fast rate, but it's very expensive.
- **Low pressure** less expensive, but produces a low yield at a slow rate.
- **Low temperature** produces a high yield but the reaction is very slow.
- **High temperature** fast reaction, but a low yield is produced.

The conditions have to be chosen very carefully so that they are economically viable **and** can meet demand. So, a compromise solution is reached:

- Pressure = 200 atmospheres.
- Temperature = 450°C.

HT Closed Systems

In a **closed system**, no reactants are added and no products are removed.

When a reversible reaction occurs in a closed system, an equilibrium is achieved when the reactions occur at exactly the **same rate** in **each direction**.

The relative amounts of all the reacting substances at equilibrium depend on the conditions of the reaction.

Look at this reaction:

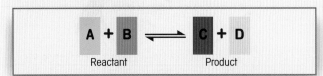

If the forward reaction (the reaction that produces the products C and D) is **endothermic** then...

- if the temperature is increased the yield of products is increased

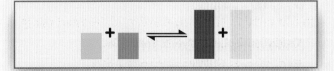

- if the temperature is decreased the yield of products is decreased

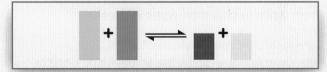

If the forward reaction is **exothermic** then...

- if the temperature is increased the yield of products is decreased

- if the temperature is decreased the yield of products is increased

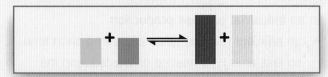

Even though a reversible reaction may not go to completion, it may still be used efficiently in an industrial process.

State Symbols

State symbols are used in equations. The symbols are **(s) solid, (l) liquid, (g) gas** and **(aq) aqueous**.

An **aqueous solution** is produced when a substance is **dissolved in water**.

Electrolysis

Electrolysis is the **breaking down** of a compound containing **ions**, into its **elements** using an **electrical current**.

Ionic substances are chemical compounds that allow an **electric current** to flow through them when they are…

* molten
* dissolved in water.

These compounds contain **negative** and **positive** ions. During electrolysis…

* **negatively charged ions** move to the **positive electrode**
* **positively charged ions** move to the **negative electrode**.

When this happens, simpler substances are released at the two electrodes.

This moving of electrons forms electrically **neutral** atoms or molecules which are then released.

If there is a **mixture of ions** in the solution, the products formed depend on the reactivity of the elements involved.

For example, in the electrolysis of **copper chloride solution**, the simple substances released are…

* copper at the negative electrode
* chlorine gas at the positive electrode.

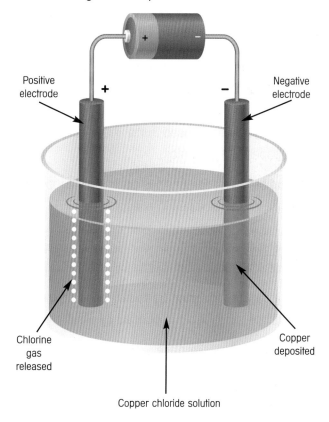

Positive electrode

Negative electrode

Chlorine gas released

Copper deposited

Copper chloride solution

Redox Reactions

Reduction is when **positively** charged ions **gain** electrons at the **negative** electrode.

Oxidation is when **negatively** charged ions **lose** electrons at the **positive** electrode.

A **redox** reaction is a chemical reaction where **both** **reduction** and **oxidation** occur.

You can remember this by thinking of the word **oilrig**:

* **O**xidation **I**s **L**oss of electrons (**OIL**)
* **R**eduction **I**s **G**ain of electrons (**RIG**)

Key Words

Current • Electrode • Electrolysis • Equilibrium • Ion • Oxidation • Reduction

Electrolysis

Electrolysis of Sodium Chloride Solution

Sodium chloride (common salt) is a compound of an alkali metal and a halogen. It is found in large quantities in the sea and in underground deposits.

Electrolysis of sodium chloride solution (brine) produces some important reagents for the chemical industry…
- **chlorine gas** (at the positive **electrode**)
- **hydrogen gas** (at the negative electrode)
- **sodium hydroxide solution** (passed out of the cell).

Chlorine is used to kill bacteria in drinking water and swimming pools, and to manufacture hydrochloric acid, disinfectants, bleach and PVC.

Hydrogen is used in the manufacture of ammonia and margarine.

Sodium hydroxide is used in the manufacture of soap, paper and ceramics.

Chlorine bleaches damp litmus paper. This is how its presence can be detected in a laboratory.

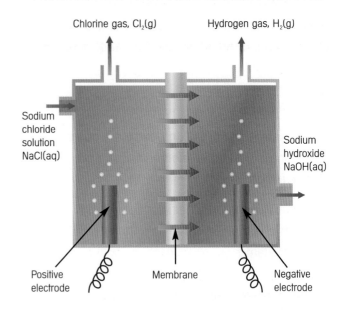

| Sodium chloride | + | Water | $\xrightarrow{\text{electrolysis}}$ | Hydrogen | + | Chlorine | + | Sodium hydroxide |

$$2NaCl(aq) + 2H_2O(l) \longrightarrow H_2(g) + Cl_2(g) + 2NaOH(aq)$$

Purification of Copper by Electrolysis

Copper can be **extracted by** reduction, but when it is needed in a pure form it is **purified by** electrolysis.

For electrolysis to take place…
- the positive electrode needs to be made of impure copper
- the negative electrode needs to be made of pure copper
- the solution must contain copper ions.

When an electrical current is passed into the solution, copper **ions** from the **positive electrode** pass into the solution and move towards the negative electrode.

At the **negative electrode**, the copper ions become **copper atoms** which stick to the pure copper electrode.

So, the negative electrode gets bigger, whilst the positive electrode seems to dissolve away and the impurities fall to the bottom of the solution.

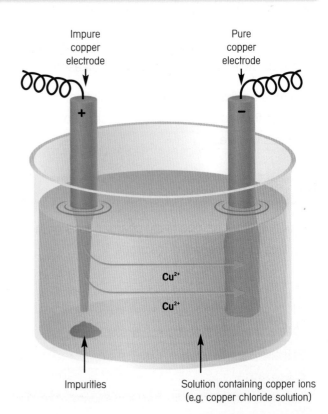

HT Electrolysis Equations

Reactions that occur at the electrodes during electrolysis can be represented by **half-equations**.

For example, in the electrolysis of copper…
- copper is deposited at the **negative electrode**

$$Cu^{2+} + 2e^- \longrightarrow Cu(s)$$

- chlorine gas is given off at the positive electrode. (Remember that chlorine exists as molecules.)

$$2Cl^- + 2e^- \longrightarrow Cl_2(g)$$

N.B. When writing equations, remember to include the state symbols.

Indicators and pH Scale

Indicators are dyes which change colour depending on whether they are in **acidic** or **alkaline** solutions:
- **Litmus** is an indicator which changes colour from red to blue or *vice versa*.
- **Universal indicator** is a mixture of dyes which show a **range** of colours to indicate **how** acidic or alkaline a substance is.

The **pH scale** is a measure of the **acidity or alkalinity** of an **aqueous solution**, across a **14-point scale**. When substances dissolve in water, they dissociate into their individual ions:
- Hydroxide ions, OH⁻(aq), make solutions alkaline.
- Hydrogen ions, H⁺(aq), make solutions acidic.

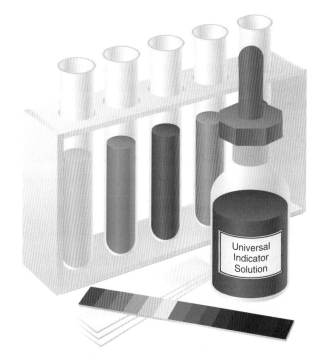

Universal Indicator Solution

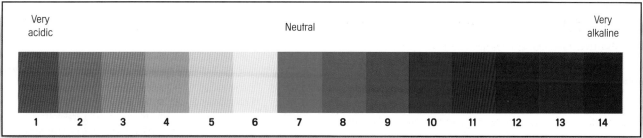

Very acidic						Neutral							Very alkaline
1	2	3	4	5	6	7	8	9	10	11	12	13	14

Key Words

Acid • Alkali • Electrode • Electrolysis • Ion • pH • Reduction

Neutralisation

Neutralisation

Acids and alkalis are chemical opposites:

- **Acids** contain **hydrogen ions**, $H^+(aq)$.
- **Alkalis** contain **hydroxide ions**, $OH^-(aq)$.

If they are added together in the correct amounts they can 'cancel out' each other.

When an acid reacts with an alkali, the **ions** react together to produce **water** (pH 7).

$$H^+(aq) \;+\; OH^-(aq) \longrightarrow H_2O(l)$$

This type of reaction is called **neutralisation** because the solution that remains has a pH of 7, showing it is neutral. For example, hydrochloric acid and potassium hydroxide can be neutralised.

Hydrochloric acid	+	Potassium hydroxide	→	Potassium chloride	+	Water
$HCl(l)$	+	$KOH(l)$	→	$KCl(s)$	+	$H_2O(l)$

Neutralising HCl and KOH

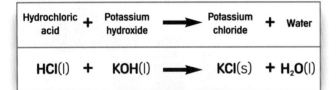

HCl (containing universal indicator) — pH 1

KOH (containing universal indicator) — pH 14

KCl + H₂O (containing universal indicator) — pH 7

Neutralising Ammonia

Ammonia is an **alkaline gas** which dissolves in water to make an **alkaline solution**.

It is mainly used in the production of fertilisers to increase the nitrogen content of the soil.

Ammonia neutralises nitric acid to produce **ammonium nitrate**. The aqueous ammonium nitrate is then evaporated to dryness.

Ammonia	+	Nitric acid	→	Ammonium nitrate
$NH_3(aq)$	+	$HNO_3(aq)$	→	$NH_4NO_3(aq)$

Ammonium nitrate, a fertiliser rich in nitrogen, is also known as 'nitram' (nitrate of ammonia). **Nitrogen-based fertilisers** are important chemicals because they increase the yields of crops.

But, nitrates can create problems if they find their way into streams, rivers or groundwater. They can…

- upset the natural balance of water
- contaminate our drinking water.

Ammonium can be neutralised with acids to produce ammonium salts.

	Hydrochloric Acid	Sulfuric Acid	Nitric Acid
Ammonium Hydroxide	Ammonium chloride and water	Ammonium sulfate and water	Ammonium nitrate and water

Key Words

Acid • Alkali • Insoluble • Ion • Neutralisation • Precipitation • Salt

Forming Salts

Soluble Salts from Metals

Metals react with dilute acid to form a **metal salt** and **hydrogen**.

Salt is a word used to describe any metal compound made from a reaction between a metal and an acid.

Some metals react with acid more vigorously than others:
- Silver – no reaction.
- Zinc – fairly reasonable reaction.
- Magnesium – vigorous reaction.
- Potassium – very violent and dangerous reaction.

Soluble Salts from Insoluble Bases

Bases are the oxides and hydroxides of metals. Soluble bases are called **alkalis**.

The oxides and hydroxides of transition metals are **insoluble**. Their salts are prepared in the following way:

1 The metal oxide or hydroxide is added to an acid until no more will react.

2 The excess metal oxide or hydroxide is then filtered, leaving a solution of the salt.

3 The salt solution is then evaporated.

This reaction can be written generally as…

Example

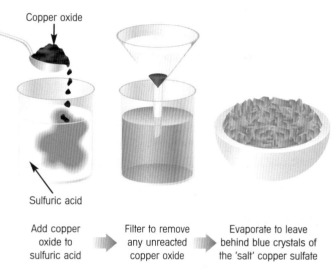

Copper oxide

Sulfuric acid

| Add copper oxide to sulfuric acid | Filter to remove any unreacted copper oxide | Evaporate to leave behind blue crystals of the 'salt' copper sulfate |

Salts of Alkali Metals

Compounds of alkali metals, called **salts**, can be made by reacting solutions of their hydroxides (which are alkaline) with a particular acid. This neutralisation reaction can be represented as follows…

The salt produced depends on the metal in the alkali and the acid used.

	Hydrochloric Acid	Sulfuric Acid	Nitric Acid
Sodium Hydroxide	Sodium chloride and water	Sodium sulfate and water	Sodium nitrate and water
Potassium Hydroxide	Potassium chloride and water	Potassium sulfate and water	Potassium nitrate and water

Insoluble Salts

Insoluble salts can be made by mixing appropriate solutions of ions so that a precipitate (solid substance) is formed.

Precipitation can be used to remove unwanted ions from a solution, e.g. softening hard water. The calcium (or magnesium) ions are precipitated out as insoluble calcium (or magnesium) carbonate.

Unit 2 Summary

Atoms

Nucleus = protons (positive) + neutrons (no charge).

Nucleus surrounded by electrons (negative). Atom has no overall charge.

Isotopes = atoms of the same element with different number of neutrons.

Atomic number = number of protons in an atom.

Mass number = number of protons and neutrons in an atom.

Atoms are arranged in the periodic table in **groups** and **periods**. Alkali metals = 1 electron in the outer shell. Halogens = 7 electrons in the outer shell. When atoms form chemical bonds, their outer shell of electrons changes.

(HT) **Relative atomic mass** (A_r) = the mass of a particular atom (compared with a twelfth of the mass of a carbon atom).

Relative formula mass (M_r) = the relative atomic masses of all the elements added together.

Compound = two or more elements chemically combined together.

Mixture = two or more elements or compounds not chemically combined.

Ionic and Covalent Bonds

Ionic compounds = giant structures held together by strong forces of attraction between oppositely charged ions.

Ionic bonds = between metal and non-metal atoms ▶ electrons are transferred

Covalent bonds = non-metal atoms ▶ electrons are shared

Giant covalent structures = strong, covalent bonds and high melting points, e.g. diamond, graphite, silicon dioxide.

(HT) Metals can conduct heat and electricity because they have **delocalised electrons**.

Moles

A **mole** = measure of the number of particles contained in a substance.

Element ▶ mass of one mole = **relative atomic mass**.

Compound ▶ mass of one mole = **relative formula mass**.

Yield and Atom Economy

Atoms are never lost or gained in a chemical reaction.

Atom economy = measure of the starting materials that end up as useful products.

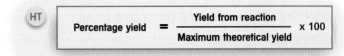

(HT)
$$\text{Percentage yield} = \frac{\text{Yield from reaction}}{\text{Maximum theoretical yield}} \times 100$$

Reversible Reactions

Reversible reaction:

$$A + B \underset{endothermic}{\overset{exothermic}{\rightleftharpoons}} C + D$$

The Haber process = nitrogen + hydrogen ➡ ammonia

HT Both demand and economic viability have to be considered in the Haber process. A compromise of 200 atmospheres pressure and 450°C are used.

Reversible reaction occurs in a closed system ➡ **equilibrium** achieved when the reactions occur at the same rate in the same direction.

Chemical Reactions

Activation energy = minimum amount of energy required to cause a reaction.

Reaction rates can be affected by temperature, concentration, surface area and use of a catalyst. Reaction rates can be found by measuring the amount of reactants used, or measuring the amount of products formed.

- **Exothermic** reactions **give out** heat.
- **Endothermic** reactions **take in** heat.

HT **Exothermic** reaction ➡ raised temperatures decrease yields ➡ lowered temperatures increase yields.

Endothermic reaction ➡ raised temperatures increase yields ➡ lowered temperatures decrease yields.

Electrolysis

Electrolysis = breaking down of an ionic compound into its elements using an electrical current.

Negative ions ➡ positive electrode

Positive ions ➡ negative electrode

Copper can be purified by electrolysis. The electrolysis of sodium chloride solution produces...
- chlorine gas at the positive electrode
- hydrogen gas at the negative electrode
- sodium hydroxide solution.

Neutralisation and Forming Salts

Acid + Alkali = neutral solutions

Metals react with dilute acid to form a metal salt and hydrogen. Compounds of alkali metals can be made by reacting solutions of their hydroxides.

Unit 2 Practice Questions

1 There are four parts to this question. For each part, tick the correct answer.

The following information describes the structure of the sodium atom. Use this information to answer the questions that follow.

$^{23}_{11}Na$

a) Which subatomic particle does ✚ represent?

i) Electron ☐ **ii)** Neutron ☐

iii) Proton ☐ **iv)** Nucleus ☐

b) How many neutrons does an atom of sodium have?

i) 1 ☐ **ii)** 23 ☐

iii) 11 ☐ **iv)** 12 ☐

c) Which group of the Periodic Table does sodium belong to?

i) Group 1 ☐ **ii)** Group 4 ☐

iii) Group 5 ☐ **iv)** Group 7 ☐

d) What kind of ion will an atom of sodium produce?

i) Positive ☐ **ii)** Negative ☐

iii) Neutral ☐ **iv)** Radioactive ☐

2 Ammonia is prepared in industry by reacting the raw materials hydrogen and nitrogen. The reaction is shown as: $N_2 + 3H_2 \rightleftharpoons 2NH_3$

a) What do the arrows ⇌ show about the reaction? ....

b) The reaction to make ammonia is **exothermic**. What does exothermic mean?

....

c) Give the sources of the following two reactants…

Nitrogen: .... Hydrogen: ....

d) Explain why a high pressure helps the formation of ammonia.

....

e) A catalyst is used to help the formation of ammonia.

i) What is the name of the catalyst used? ....

ii) Why is a catalyst used? ....

3 Sodium hydroxide (NaOH) is also known as caustic soda.

a) Calculate the relative formula mass (M_r) of sodium hydroxide. (A_r: Na = 23, H = 1, O = 16.)

....

b) Calculate the percentage of oxygen in sodium hydroxide.

....

c) Calculate the mass of oxygen in 5g of sodium hydroxide.

....

d) Calculate the mass of 4 moles of sodium hydroxide.

....

4 a) Diamond and graphite are different forms of carbon. Explain, with reference to the arrangement of carbon atoms, why diamond is a very hard substance.

....

b) Give one property of silicon dioxide that both diamond and graphite have.

....

5 The diagram shows the apparatus used for the electrolysis of copper chloride solution.

a) Name the gas produced at the positive electrode.

....

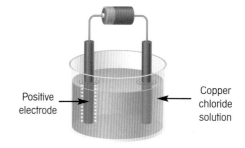

Positive electrode

Copper chloride solution

b) Why do copper ions move to the negative electrode?

....

....

c) What is the difference between reduction and oxidation in terms of electrons?

....

6 a) Complete the following word equations which show the formation of salts.

i) Hydrochloric acid + Potassium hydroxide ⟶ .... + Water

ii) .... + Copper oxide ⟶ Copper sulfate + Water

iii) Nitric acid + ... ⟶ Sodium nitrate + Water

iv) Barium chloride + Zinc sulfate ⟶ .... + ...

b) What is the name of the only insoluble salt in the equations above? ....

The Periodic Table

Early Attempts to Classify the Elements

Several attempts have been made to group the elements in a table.

When **John Newlands** tried to arrange a periodic table in 1864, only 63 elements were known about; many were still **undiscovered**.

Newlands arranged the known elements in order of their **atomic weights** and found similar properties amongst every eighth element in the series. (This makes sense since the noble gases (Group 8) weren't discovered until 1894.)

He noticed periodicity (repeated patterns) although the missing elements caused problems.

But, strictly following the order of **atomic weight** created problems because it meant some of the elements were placed in the **wrong group**.

Dimitri Mendeleev realised that some elements had yet to be discovered, so when he created his table in 1869 he left **gaps** to allow for their discovery. He used his periodic table to predict the existence of other elements.

The Modern Periodic Table

The discovery of **subatomic particles** (protons, neutrons and electrons) and **electronic structure** provided further evidence which could be used to create a table. The periodic table was then arranged in order of atomic (proton) numbers. So, the modern periodic table is an arrangement of the elements in terms of their **electronic structure**.

The elements are arranged in **periods** (rows) according to the **number of electrons** in their outer **energy level** (shell). From left to right across each period,

an energy level is gradually filled with electrons. In the next period, the next energy level is filled, etc.

This arrangement means elements with the same number of electrons in their outer energy level are in the same **group** (column), e.g. Group 1 elements have 1 electron in their outer energy level. Elements that have the **same number of electrons** in their outer energy level have **similar properties**.

The table is called a **periodic table** because similar properties occur at **regular intervals**.

1	2											3	4	5	6	7	8 or 0
							1 **H** hydrogen 1										4 **He** helium 2
7 **Li** lithium 3	9 **Be** beryllium 4											11 **B** boron 5	12 **C** carbon 6	14 **N** nitrogen 7	16 **O** oxygen 8	19 **F** fluorine 9	20 **Ne** neon 10
23 **Na** sodium 11	24 **Mg** magnesium 12											27 **Al** aluminium 13	28 **Si** silicon 14	31 **P** phosphorus 15	32 **S** sulfur 16	35.5 **Cl** chlorine 17	40 **Ar** argon 18
39 **K** potassium 19	40 **Ca** calcium 20	45 **Sc** scandium 21	48 **Ti** titanium 22	51 **V** vanadium 23	52 **Cr** chromium 24	55 **Mn** manganese 25	56 **Fe** iron 26	59 **Co** cobalt 27	59 **Ni** nickel 28	63.5 **Cu** copper 29	65 **Zn** zinc 30	70 **Ga** gallium 31	73 **Ge** germanium 32	75 **As** arsenic 33	79 **Se** selenium 34	80 **Br** bromine 35	84 **Kr** krypton 36
85 **Rb** rubidium 37	88 **Sr** strontium 38	89 **Y** yttrium 39	91 **Zr** zirconium 40	93 **Nb** niobium 41	96 **Mo** molybdenum 42	[98] **Tc** technetium 43	101 **Ru** ruthenium 44	103 **Rh** rhodium 45	106 **Pd** palladium 46	108 **Ag** silver 47	112 **Cd** cadmium 48	115 **In** indium 49	119 **Sn** tin 50	122 **Sb** antimony 51	128 **Te** tellurium 52	127 **I** iodine 53	131 **Xe** xenon 54
133 **Cs** caesium 55	137 **Ba** barium 56	139 **La*** lanthanum 57	178 **Hf** hafnium 72	181 **Ta** tantalum 73	184 **W** tungsten 74	186 **Re** rhenium 75	190 **Os** osmium 76	192 **Ir** iridium 77	195 **Pt** platinum 78	197 **Au** gold 79	201 **Hg** mercury 80	204 **Tl** thallium 81	207 **Pb** lead 82	209 **Bi** bismuth 83	[209] **Po** polonium 84	[210] **At** astatine 85	[222] **Rn** radon 86
[223] **Fr** francium 87	[226] **Ra** radium 88	[227] **Ac*** actinium 89	[261] **Rf** rutherfordium 104	[262] **Db** dubnium 105	[266] **Sg** seaborgium 106	[264] **Bh** bohrium 107	[277] **Hs** hassium 108	[268] **Mt** meitnerium 109	[271] **Ds** darmstadtium 110	[272] **Rg** roentgenium 111							

Group 1 – The Alkali Metals

There are six elements in **Group 1**. They are known as the **alkali metals**.

Alkali metals…

* have **low** melting and boiling points that **decrease** as you go down the group
* have a **low** density (lithium, sodium and potassium are less dense than water)
* become **more reactive** as you go down the group.

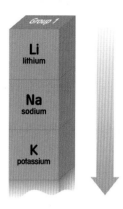

Reactivity increases, and melting and boiling points decrease as you go down the group.

HT Trends in Group 1

Alkali metals have **similar properties** to each other because they have the same number of electrons in their outer energy level, i.e. the highest occupied energy level in an atom of each element contains **1 electron**.

Alkali metals become **more reactive** as you go down the group because the outer energy level gets further away from the influence of the nucleus, and so an **electron is lost more easily**.

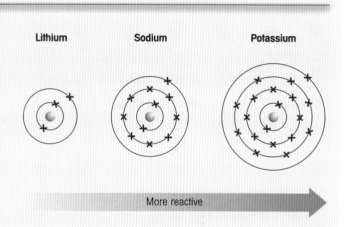

Lithium   Sodium   Potassium

More reactive

Reactions of Alkali Metals

The alkali metals are stored under oil because they react very vigorously with oxygen and water. When alkali metals react with **water**, a **metal hydroxide** is formed and **hydrogen** gas is given off. For example…

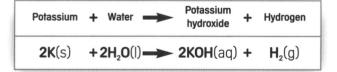

Potassium	+	Water	➡	Potassium hydroxide	+	Hydrogen
2K(s)		+ **2H$_2$O**(l) ➡		**2KOH**(aq) +		**H$_2$**(g)

If a metal hydroxide (e.g. potassium hydroxide) is **dissolved** in water, an **alkaline solution** is produced.

Alkali metals react with **non-metals** to form **ionic compounds**. When this happens, the metal atom **loses** one electron to form a metal ion with a **positive charge** (+1). The products are **white solids** that **dissolve** in water to form **colourless** solutions.

Alkali Metals Reacting with Water

Li   Na   K

Key Words

Alkali • Electron • Electronic structure • Ionic compound • Neutron • Proton

The Periodic Table

Group 7 – The Halogens

There are five **elements** in Group 7. They are known as the **halogens**. They are non-metals.

The halogens…

- have melting and boiling points that **increase** as you go down the group (at room temperature, fluorine and chlorine are gases, and bromine is a liquid)
- have **coloured vapours** (chlorine's and bromine's vapours smell particularly strong)
- exist as **molecules** made up of **pairs of atoms**
- become **less reactive** as you go down the group.

Reactivity decreases, and melting and boiling points increase as you go down the group.

HT Trends in Group 7

Halogens have **similar properties** because they have the same number of electrons (i.e. 7) in their outer energy level.

They become less reactive as you go down the group because the outer energy level gets further away from the influence of the nucleus, and so an electron **is gained less easily**.

The more energy levels an atom has…
- the more easily electrons are lost
- the less easily electrons are gained.

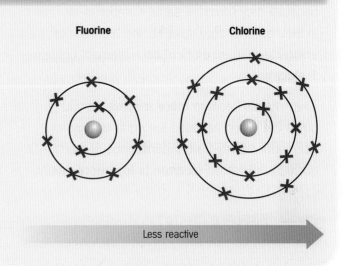

Reaction of Halogens

Halogens react with **metals** to produce **ionic salts**. The **halogen atom gains** one electron to form a **halide ion** (i.e. a chloride, bromide or iodide ion) which carries a **negative charge** (-1). For example…

Lithium	+	Chlorine	→	Lithium chloride
$2Li(s)$	+	$Cl_2(g)$	→	$2LiCl(s)$

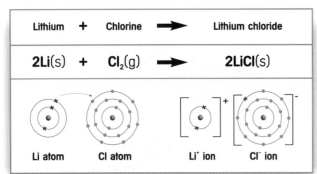

Halogens react with other **non-metallic** elements to form **molecular compounds**, for example:

Hydrogen	+	Chlorine	→	Hydrogen chloride
$2H(g)$	+	$Cl_2(g)$	→	$2HCl(g)$

A more reactive halogen will **displace** a less reactive halogen from an aqueous solution of its salt, i.e.…
- chlorine will displace both bromine and iodine
- bromine will displace iodine.

The Transition Metals

In the **centre** of the periodic table, between Groups 2 and 3, is a block of metallic elements called the **transition metals** (or **transition elements**).

Many transition metals...
- form **coloured compounds**
- have **ions** with **different charges**, e.g. Fe^{2+} and Fe^{3+}
- can be used as catalysts to speed up chemical reactions.

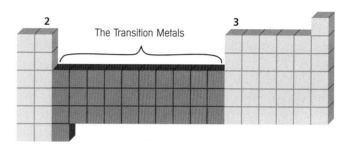

The Transition Metals

Properties of Transition Metals

Like all other metals, transition metals...
- are good **conductors** of heat and electricity
- can be **easily bent** or **hammered** into shape.

In comparison to Group 1 metals, transition metals...
- have higher densities and high melting points (except mercury, which is liquid at room temperature)
- are hard and mechanically strong (except mercury)
- are much **less reactive** and don't react as vigorously with oxygen or water.

HT The transition elements have **similar properties** to each other. They also have some special properties because a lower energy level (inner shell) is being filled in the atoms of these elements.

This is because the third energy level can hold up to **18 electrons** once 2 electrons have occupied the fourth energy level.

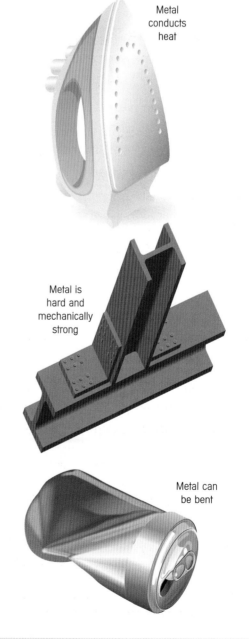

Metal conducts heat

Metal is hard and mechanically strong

Metal can be bent

Key Words

Catalyst • Compound • Salt

Acids and Alkalis

Acids and Alkalis

Some **compounds** react with water to produce **acidic** or **alkaline** **solutions**. These compounds might not exhibit any acidic or alkaline characteristics on their own. They need **water** to be present to be able to act as an **acid** or a **base**.

All **acids** in aqueous solution **dissociate** to produce **hydrogen** **ions** (H^+). The hydrogen ion is a proton that is hydrated in water (i.e. chemically bonded to water) and is represented as $H^+(aq)$. The presence of hydrogen ions gives a solution its acidic characteristics, for example, hydrochloric acid contains hydrogen ions:

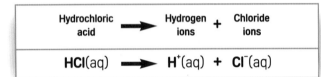

Hydrochloric acid	$\longrightarrow$	Hydrogen ions	+	Chloride ions
$HCl(aq)$	$\longrightarrow$	$H^+(aq)$	+	$Cl^-(aq)$

All **alkalis** in aqueous solution **dissociate** to produce **hydroxide ions** (OH^-).

The presence of hydroxide ions gives a solution its alkaline characteristics, for example, sodium hydroxide contains hydroxide ions:

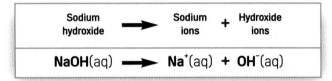

Sodium hydroxide	$\longrightarrow$	Sodium ions	+	Hydroxide ions
$NaOH(aq)$	$\longrightarrow$	$Na^+(aq)$	+	$OH^-(aq)$

HT An acid can be defined as a **proton donor** and a base can be defined as a **proton acceptor**. But, an acid cannot donate a proton unless there is an appropriate base available to accept it.

Strength of Acids and Alkalis

Acids and alkalis are **classified** by the **extent** of their **ionisation** in water:

- A **strong** acid or alkali is one that is completely ionised in water, i.e. all of the compound dissociates into ions.
- A **weak** acid or alkali, is one that is only partially ionised in water, i.e. not all of the compound dissociates into ions.

	Strong	Weak
Acid	• Hydrochloric acid • Sulfuric acid • Nitric acid	• Ethanoic acid • Citric acid • Carbonic acid
Alkali	• Sodium hydroxide • Potassium hydroxide	• Ammonia solution

Key Words

Acid • Alkali • Compound • Dissociate •
Ion • Neutralisation • Titration

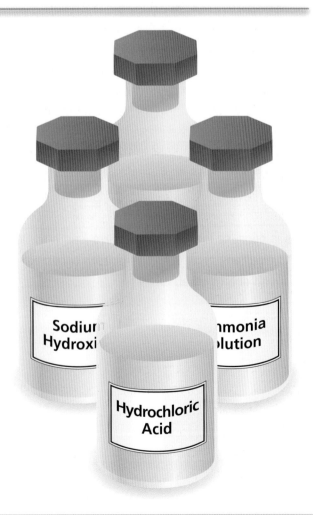

Titration

Titration is an accurate technique that you can use to find out **how much** of an **acid** is needed to neutralise an alkali.

When **neutralisation** takes place, the hydrogen ions (H^+) from the acid join with the hydroxide ions (OH^-) from the alkali to form water (neutral pH).

Hydrogen ion	+	Hydroxide ion	→	Water molecule
$H^+(aq)$	+	$OH^-(aq)$	→	$H_2O(l)$

Use this titration method:

1. Wash and rinse a pipette with the alkali that you will use.
2. Use the pipette to measure out a known and accurate volume of the alkali.
3. Place the alkali in a clean, dry conical flask. Add a suitable indicator, e.g. phenolphthalein.
4. Place the acid in a burette that has been carefully washed and rinsed with the acid. Take a reading of the volume of acid in the burette (initial reading).
5. Carefully add the acid to the alkali until the indicator changes colour to show neutrality. This is called the **end point**. Take a reading of the volume of acid in the burette (final reading).
6. Calculate the volume of acid added (i.e. subtract the final reading from the initial reading).

The method can be repeated to check results and can then be performed without an indicator in order to obtain the salt.

Clamp

Burette

Acid

Conical flask

Alkali and indicator

White tile (allows you to see the colour change clearly)

Indicators

Different strength acids and alkalis can react together to form a neutral solution. You must use a suitable **indicator** in titrations:

- Strong acid + strong alkali
  - use any suitable acid–base indicator (e.g. universal, litmus).

(HT) Other indicators are required for different concentrations:

- Strong acid + weak alkali
  - use methyl orange indicator.
- Weak acid + strong alkali
  - use phenolphthalein indicator.

Titration

Titration can be used to find the **concentration** of an **acid** or **alkali** providing you know either…
- the relative **volumes** of acid and alkali used **or**
- the **concentration** of the other acid or alkali.

It will help if you break down the calculation:

1 Write down a **balanced equation** for the reaction to determine the ratio of moles of acid to alkali involved.

2 Calculate the number of moles in the solution of known volume and concentration. (You will know the number of moles in the other solution from your previous calculation.)

3 Calculate the concentration of the other solution using this formula:

$$\text{Concentration of solution (mol dm}^{-3}\text{ or M)} = \frac{\text{Number of moles of solute (mol)}}{\text{Volume of solution (dm}^{-3}\text{)}}$$

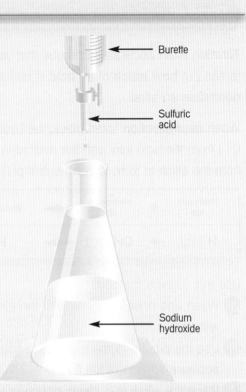

Burette

Sulfuric acid

Sodium hydroxide

Example 1

A titration is carried out and 0.04dm^3 hydrochloric acid neutralises 0.08dm^3 sodium hydroxide of concentration 1mol dm^{-3}. Calculate the concentration of the hydrochloric acid.

Write the balanced symbol equation for the reaction.

$$HCl(aq) + NaOH(aq) \longrightarrow NaCl(aq) + H_2O(l)$$

You can see that 1 mole of HCl neutralises 1 mole of NaOH. So rearrange the formula.

$$\text{Number of moles of NaOH} = \text{Concentration of NaOH} \times \text{Volume of NaOH}$$

$$= 1\text{mol dm}^{-3} \times 0.08\text{dm}^3$$
$$= 0.08\text{mol}$$

Number of moles of HCl used up in the reaction is also 0.08mol. Now calculate the concentration of HCl.

$$\text{Concentration of HCl} = \frac{\text{Number of moles of HCl (mol)}}{\text{Volume of HCl (dm}^3\text{)}}$$

$$= \frac{0.08\text{mol}}{0.04\text{dm}^3}$$

$$= \textbf{2mol dm}^{-3}$$

Example 2

A titration is carried out and 0.035dm^3 sulfuric acid of concentration 0.6mol dm^{-3} neutralises 0.14dm^3 sodium hydroxide. Calculate the concentration of the sodium hydroxide.

Write the balanced symbol equation for the reaction.

$$H_2SO_4(aq) + 2NaOH(aq) \longrightarrow Na_2SO_4(aq) + 2H_2O(l)$$

This time, 1 mole of H_2SO_4 neutralises 2 moles of NaOH.

$$\text{Number of moles of H}_2\text{SO}_4 = \text{Concentration of H}_2\text{SO}_4 \times \text{Volume of H}_2\text{SO}_4$$

$$= 0.6\text{mol dm}^{-3} \times 0.035\text{dm}^3$$
$$= \textbf{0.021 mol}$$

Calculate the number of moles of NaOH used up in the reaction. Then calculate the concentration of NaOH.

$$2 \times 0.021 = \textbf{0.042mol.}$$

$$\text{Concentration of NaOH} = \frac{\text{Number of moles of NaOH (mol)}}{\text{Volume of NaOH (dm}^3\text{)}}$$

$$= \frac{0.042\text{mol}}{0.14\text{dm}^3}$$

$$= \textbf{0.3mol dm}^{-3}$$

The Importance of Water

Water is the most abundant substance on the surface of the Earth and it's **essential** for the existence of all **life**.

Water is an important raw material and can be used...
- as a solvent where substances are dissolved in it
- as a **coolant** to remove heat from a system
- in many **industrial processes** (including in the manufacture of sulfuric acid).

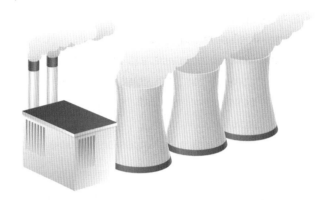

The Water Cycle

The Sun provides the **energy** that drives the water cycle. Heat energy from the Sun causes water in rivers, lakes and oceans to rise by **evaporation**.

The water vapour cools as it rises higher and higher into the atmosphere, and **condensation** occurs, forming droplets of water which collect together to form clouds.

As the clouds rise higher, the **temperature drops** further and **rain** is produced when the droplets are big enough. **Snow** is produced when clouds rise further still and get even colder.

The rain (or snow) then **falls** onto the land, drains into rivers and **flows** into the sea, and the cycle begins again.

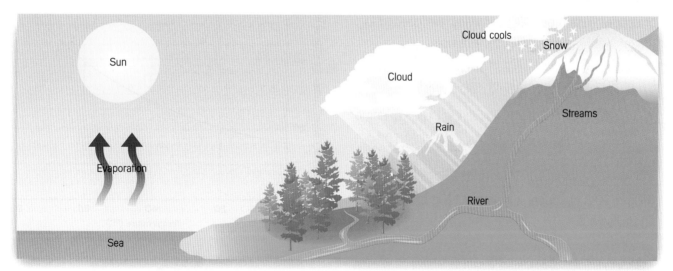

Dissolving Substances in Water

If a solid dissolves in water it is said to be soluble. The solid which dissolves is called the solute, and water is described as the solvent. Water is called the **universal solvent** as so many substances dissolve in it.

The solubility of a solute in water is usually given in grams of solute per 100 grams of water (g/100g of water) at a specific temperature.

Key Words
Solubility • Soluble • Solute • Solvent

Dissolving Substances in Water

Solubility of Compounds

The type of compound a substance is determines whether it is **soluble** or insoluble:

- Most **ionic compounds**, e.g. sodium chloride and copper sulfate, are **soluble** in water.
- Most **covalent compounds**, e.g. silicon dioxide, are **insoluble** in water.
- Some **molecular substances** are **soluble**.

The temperature of the **solvent** plays an important part in **solubility**, i.e. how much **solute** can be dissolved in a solvent. The **solubility** of most solutes **increases** as the **temperature increases**.

A **solubility curve** shows the **maximum** amount of solute that dissolves in a solvent at a particular temperature to give a saturated solution. For example, this graph shows a solubility curve for copper sulfate in 100g of water.

You can use the graph to find out how many grams of copper sulfate per 100g of water are needed to make a saturated solution, for example…

- at 20°C it's 20g/100g of water
- at 60°C it's 40g/100g of water.

When a warm saturated solution cools down, some of the solute will separate from the solution and **crystallise** out. For example, if the copper sulfate solution is cooled down from 60°C to 20°C, then 20g (40g − 20g) of copper sulfate per 100g of water will crystallise out.

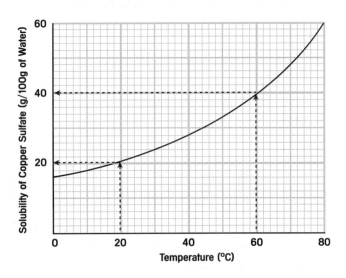

Solubility of Gases

Many **gases** are **soluble** in **water**. The **solubility** of a gas **increases** as…

- the **temperature** of the water is **lowered**
- **pressure** is **increased**.

Dissolving **carbon dioxide** under high pressure produces carbonated water, which is used in fizzy drinks such as lemonade. Unscrewing the bottle top releases the pressure and results in carbon dioxide bubbling out of the solution.

Oxygen dissolves in water; this dissolved oxygen is essential for aquatic life. But, as the temperature of the water is increased, the amount of oxygen that can be dissolved in it decreases.

For example, the discharge of hot water from power stations reduces the amount of oxygen dissolved in the water, which can damage aquatic life.

Hard and Soft Water

Drinking Water

Water of the correct quality is **essential** for **life**.

Water naturally contains **microorganisms** and **dissolved** salts.

Water that is good quality and safe to drink is produced as follows:

1. The water is passed through a **filter bed** to remove any solid particles.
2. **Chlorine gas** is then added to kill any harmful microorganisms.

To improve the taste and quality of tap water, more dissolved substances can be removed by passing the water through a **filter** containing carbon, silver and ion **exchange resins**.

Any water can be distilled to produce **pure water**, i.e. water that contains no dissolved substances. The water is boiled to produce steam, which is condensed by cooling it to produce pure liquid water. This process uses a lot of energy, which makes it expensive.

Hard and Soft Water

The amount of compounds present in tap water determines whether it's described as **hard** or **soft**.

Soft water doesn't contain many dissolved compounds so it readily forms a **lather** with soap.

Most **hard water** contains calcium or magnesium compounds which dissolve in natural water as it flows over ground or rocks containing compounds of these elements. These dissolved substances react with soap to form **scum**, which makes it harder to form a lather.

Advantage of hard water:

- The dissolved compounds in water are **good for your health**, e.g. calcium compounds help the development of strong bones and teeth, and also help to reduce the risk of heart diseases.

Disadvantages of hard water:

- More soap is needed to form a lather, which increases costs.
- Using hard water often leads to deposits (called scale) forming in heating systems and appliances like kettles. This **reduces** their efficiency.

Removing Hardness

To make hard water soft, the **dissolved** calcium and magnesium **ions** need to be removed. This can be done in one of two ways:

- Add **sodium carbonate solution** (washing soda) to it. The carbonate ions react with the calcium and magnesium ions to form calcium carbonate and magnesium carbonate (respectively) which precipitate out of solution as they are both insoluble.
- Pass the hard water through an **ion-exchange column** which contains a resin that supplies hydrogen ions or sodium ions. As the hard water passes through the resin, the calcium and magnesium ions contained in it are replaced by hydrogen or sodium ions from the resin.

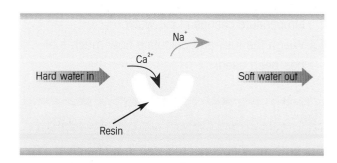

Key Words

Covalent compound • Distillation • Efficiency • Insoluble • Ion • Ionic compound • Salt • Solubility • Soluble • Solute • Solvent

Measuring Energy

Joules and Calories

The unit of measurement for **energy** is the **joule** (**J**). It takes 4.2 joules of energy to heat up 1g of water by 1°C. This amount of energy is called 1 **calorie** (**C**), i.e. 1 calorie = 4.2 joules. Information about the energy provided by food products is given in kilocalories (kcal).

Different foods provide different amounts of energy:
- Fats and oils provide large amounts of energy.
- Carbohydrates provide some energy
- Proteins provide less energy.

Eating and digesting food brings about an energy change in your body. If you eat more food than your body needs and do too little exercise, the excess energy is stored in your body in the form of **fat**.

If you continue to store fat in this way, you can become very **overweight** (**obese**). **Obesity** could lead to other illnesses such as **heart disease** and **diabetes**.

Measuring Energy by Calorimetry

When any **chemical change** takes place it is accompanied by an **energy change**, i.e. energy can be taken in or given out. The relative amounts of energy produced by food or fuels can be measured using **calorimetry**.

To measure the temperature change that takes place when a fuel burns, follow this method:
1. Place 100g of water in a calorimeter (a container made of glass or metal) and measure the temperature of the water.
2. Find the mass (in grams) of the fuel to be burned.
3. Burn the fuel under the water in the calorimeter for a few minutes.
4. Record the new temperature and calculate the temperature change of the water.
5. Weigh the fuel, and calculate how much fuel has been used.

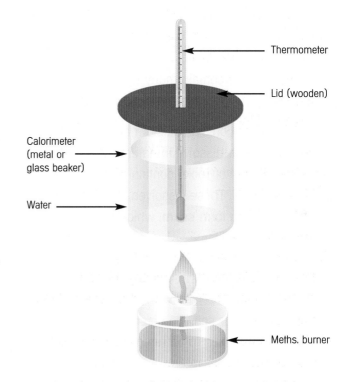

Thermometer

Lid (wooden)

Calorimeter (metal or glass beaker)

Water

Meths. burner

Measuring Energy of Chemical Reactions

The amount of energy produced in a **chemical reaction** in solution can be measured by mixing the reactants in an **insulated** container. This enables the temperature change to be measured before heat is lost to the surroundings. This method would be suitable for **neutralisation** reactions and the reactions of solids, e.g. sodium, and water.

Alkali

Acid

Making and Breaking Bonds

In a chemical reaction, new substances are produced. In order to do this, the **bonds** in the reactants must be **broken** and new bonds are **made** to form the products.

Breaking a chemical bond requires a lot of energy — this is an endothermic process.

When a new chemical bond is **formed**, energy is given out — this is an exothermic process.

If more energy is required to break old bonds than is released when the new bonds are formed, the reaction must be **endothermic**.

If more energy is released when the new bonds are formed than is needed to break the old bonds, the reaction must be **exothermic**.

Energy Level Diagrams

The energy changes in a chemical reaction can be illustrated using an **energy level diagram**:

1. In an **exothermic** reaction, energy is given out. This means energy is being lost, so the products have less energy than the reactants.
2. In an **endothermic** reaction, energy is being taken in. This means that energy is being gained, so the products have more energy than the reactants.
3. The activation energy is the energy needed to start a reaction, i.e. to break the old bonds.
4. Catalysts reduce the activation energy needed for a reaction — this makes the reaction go faster.

Key Words

Activation energy • Calorie • Catalyst • Endothermic • Energy • Exothermic • Joule • Neutralisation • Obesity

Identifying Substances

Flame Tests

Flame tests can be used to identify metal **ions**.

Lithium, sodium, potassium, calcium and barium compounds can be recognised by the distinctive colours they produce in a **flame test**.

To do a flame test, follow this method:

1. Dip a piece of nichrome (a nickel-chromium alloy) wire in concentrated hydrochloric acid to clean it.
2. Dip it in the compound.
3. Put it into a Bunsen flame. The following distinctive colours indicate the presence of certain ions:
   - apple green for **barium**
   - brick red for **calcium**
   - red for **lithium**
   - lilac for **potassium**
   - yellow for **sodium**.

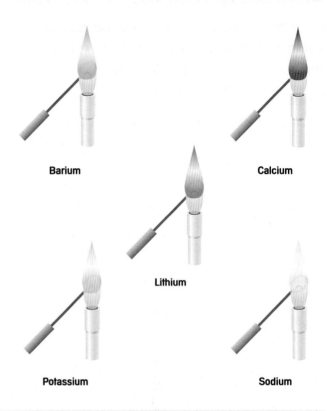

Barium

Calcium

Lithium

Potassium

Sodium

Reacting Carbonates with Dilute Acid

Carbonates react with **dilute acids** to form **carbon dioxide** gas (and a salt and water). Carbon dioxide turns limewater milky. For example…

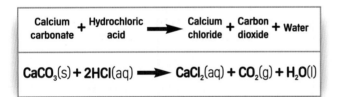

| Calcium carbonate | + | Hydrochloric acid | → | Calcium chloride | + | Carbon dioxide | + Water |

$$CaCO_3(s) + 2HCl(aq) \longrightarrow CaCl_2(aq) + CO_2(g) + H_2O(l)$$

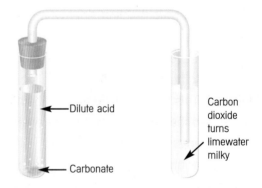

Dilute acid

Carbonate

Carbon dioxide turns limewater milky

Thermal Decomposition Reactions

When copper carbonate and zinc carbonate are heated, a **thermal decomposition** reaction takes place. This results in a distinctive colour change which enables the two compounds to be identified.

Strongly heating copper carbonate in a **combustion** tube causes it to go black as copper oxide is formed.

Strongly heating zinc carbonate in a combustion tube causes it to go yellow as zinc oxide is formed.

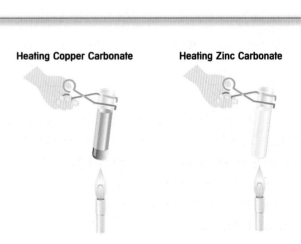

Heating Copper Carbonate

Heating Zinc Carbonate

Precipitation of Metal Ions

Metal compounds in solution contain **metal** ions. Some of these form **precipitates**, i.e. **insoluble** solids that come out of solution when sodium hydroxide solution is added to them.

For example, when sodium hydroxide solution is added to calcium chloride solution, a white precipitate of calcium hydroxide is formed (as well as sodium chloride solution). You can see how this precipitate is formed by considering the ions involved.

This table shows the precipitates formed when **metal ions** are mixed with sodium hydroxide solution.

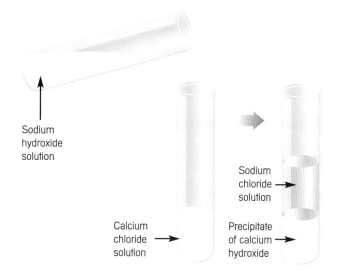

Sodium hydroxide solution

Sodium chloride solution

Calcium chloride solution

Precipitate of calcium hydroxide

Metal Ion + Sodium Hydroxide	Precipitate Formed	Colour of Precipitate
Aluminium Al^{3+}(aq) + Sodium hydroxide	Aluminium hydroxide	White
Calcium Ca^{2+}(aq) + Sodium hydroxide	Calcium hydroxide	White
Magnesium Mg^{2+}(aq) + Sodium hydroxide	Magnesium hydroxide	White
Copper Cu^{2+}(aq) + Sodium hydroxide	Copper hydroxide	Blue
Iron (II) Fe^{2+}(aq) + Sodium hydroxide	Iron (II) hydroxide	Green
Iron (III) Fe^{3+}(aq) + Sodium hydroxide	Iron (III) hydroxide	Brown

More Examples of Precipitations

If dilute hydrochloric acid and barium chloride solution are added to a solution containing **sulfate ions**, a white precipitate of barium sulfate is produced.

If sodium hydroxide is added to **ammonium ions** (NH_4^-) in solution, ammonia gas is given off. A test for ammonia gas is that it turns damp litmus paper blue.

Nitrate ions (NO_3^-) are reduced by aluminium power to form ammonia when sodium hydroxide solution is added.

Precipitates with silver nitrate solution can be produced by **halide ions** (chloride, bromide and iodide ions) in solution in the presence of dilute nitric acid:

* Silver chloride is white.
* Silver bromide is cream.
* Silver iodide is yellow.

Damp Litmus turns Blue in the Presence of Ammonia

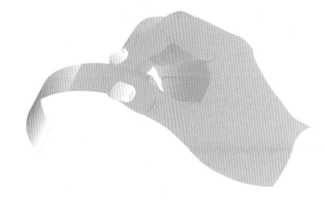

Key Words

Decomposition • Insoluble • Ion • Precipitate

Identifying Substances

Tests for Organic Compounds

The surfaces of solid organic compounds will blacken or **char** if they are burned in air. Black marks can be seen on the surface of organic compounds which are burned as carbon is made.

Bromine water can be used to identify whether **organic compounds** are saturated or unsaturated:

- If bromine water is shaken with an **unsaturated** organic compound, the bromine water changes from **brown to colourless**.
- If bromine water is shaken with a **saturated** organic compound it would **stay brown**. (This is because the bromine can't form a bond with a saturated compound.)

Unsaturated (C=C)   Saturated (C–C)

Bromine water   Bromine water

HT Empirical Formulae

The **empirical formula** of a compound shows the **ratio** of all the elements in that compound.

You can calculate the empirical formula of an organic compound by burning a known mass of the compound in oxygen and measuring the masses of all the products.

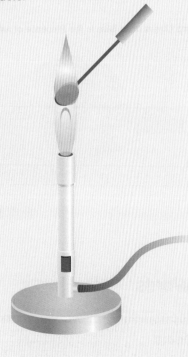

Example

11g carbon dioxide and 9g water are produced when 4g of an organic compound is burned completely in oxygen. What is the empirical formula of the compound?

> Find the mass of each element in the products, except for oxygen (which didn't come from the organic compound).

M_r of water, $H_2O = (2 \times 1) + 16 = 18$
So, water is $\frac{2}{18}$ hydrogen and $\frac{16}{18}$ oxygen.
So, the mass of hydrogen in 9g of water
$= \frac{2}{18} \times 9g = 1g$
M_r of carbon dioxide, $CO_2 = 12 + (2 \times 16) = 44$
So, carbon dioxide is $\frac{12}{44}$ carbon and $\frac{32}{44}$ oxygen.
The mass of carbon in 11g carbon dioxide
$= \frac{12}{44} \times 11g = 3g$

> Now, divide each mass by the element's atomic mass.

$H = 1 \therefore$ Hydrogen $= \frac{1}{1} = 1$ mole
$C = 12 \therefore$ Carbon $= \frac{3}{12} = 0.25$ mole

> Finally, find the ratio of one element to the other.

Ratio of hydrogen to carbon is $1 : 0.25 = 4 : 1$
So, there are 4 atoms of hydrogen to 1 atom of carbon. The empirical formula is **CH₄**.

Instrumental Methods

Standard laboratory equipment can be used to detect and **identify** elements and compounds. But, **instrumental methods** that involve using highly **accurate** instruments to analyse and identify substances have been developed to perform this function.

These instruments give rapid results, are very sensitive and accurate, and can be used on small samples.

Rapid progress in electronics and computing has provided the basis for the development of accurate instrumental methods of analysing substances. Developments in fibre optics and magnetometry have also made equipment more sophisticated.

Advances in technology have led to…
- increased miniaturisation
- greater sensitivity
- greater ease of use
- greater automation
- greater versatility.

(HT) Some instrumental methods are used to identify elements, for example, atomic absorption spectroscopy – a process used in the steel industry.

Other instrumental methods are used to identify compounds. These methods include…
- infra red spectrometry
- ultraviolet spectroscopy
- nuclear magnetic resonance spectroscopy
- gas–liquid chromatography.

Mass spectrometry measures the deflection of ions of the substance as they pass through the magnetic field of the spectrometer. It can be used to identify elements or compounds.

Key Words
Compound • Element • Saturated

Unit 3 Summary

The Periodic Table

Newlands (1864) arranged elements in atomic weights. But many elements had **not** been **discovered**. He noticed **periodicity**.

Mendeleev (1869) left **gaps** in his periodic table to allow for the discovery of other elements.

The Modern Periodic Table

Modern periodic table is arranged in terms of **electronic structure**.

Rows = periods − energy level is filled as you go across the table.

Columns = groups − with more energy levels of electrons as go down the table. All elements in a group have same number of electrons in outer shell, e.g. Group 1 = 1 electron in outer energy level.

Group	Properties	HT Explanation
Alkali metals (Group 1)	• Become more reactive as go down the group. • React vigorously with oxygen and water. • React with non-metals to form ionic compounds.	More reactive further down group because electron is further away from the influence of the nucleus so is more easily lost.
Halogens (Group 2)	• Have coloured vapours. • Become less reactive further down the group. • React with metals to produce ionic salts. • React with non-metals to form molecular compounds. • Displace less reactive halogens.	Less reactive further down the group because it is harder to attract an electron to complete the outer energy level as it gets further away from the influence of the nucleus.
Transition metals	• Form coloured compounds. • Can have ions with different charges. • Are good conductors of heat and electricity. • Are easily bent or hammered. • Can be used as catalysts.	Can hold up to 18 electrons in third energy level once 2 electrons are in fourth energy level.

Acids and Alkalis

Some compounds react with water to produce acidic or alkaline solutions:

- Acids − hydrogen ions, $H^+(aq)$.
- Alkalis − hydroxide ions, $OH^-(aq)$.

Strong acid or alkali **completely ionises** in water.
Weak acid or alkali only **partially ionises** in water.

HT Acid = proton donor.
Alkali = proton acceptor.

Titration

Titration finds out how much acid is needed to neutralise an alkali. Use different indicators depending on the strength of the acid and alkali being used.

(HT) Titration can find the concentration of an acid or alkali if you know either...
- the relative volumes of acid and alkali used **or**
- the concentration of either the acid or alkali.

Water

Water is used as a coolant, a solvent, and in many industrial applications.

Water cycle = Sun heats water →Evaporation→ Water vapour cools →Condensation→ Clouds form →Temperature drops→ Rain falls

Water can be soft or hard. Hard water contains many dissolved particles.

Water can be treated and filtered to remove microorganisms and dissolved salts.

- Ionic compounds are soluble in water.
- Covalent compounds are insoluble in water.

Solubility curve shows maximum amount of solute that can dissolve in a solvent at a given temperature.

Solubility of gases increases as temperature and/or pressure increase.

Energy

Energy measured in joules (J). Nutritional information given in kilocalories (kcal).

Chemical reactions cause an energy change:
- Heat given out = exothermic.
- Heat taken in = endothermic.

Calorimetry measures the amount of energy produced by a food.

Energy level diagrams show change in energy in a reaction.

Identifying Substances

- Flame tests identify metal ions (by colours produced).
- Carbonates give off carbon dioxide which turns limewater milky.
- Precipitation reactions of metal ions produce insoluble solids of different colours.
- Organic substances blacken or char when burned in air.
    - Unsaturated organic compounds turn bromine water colourless.
    - Saturated organic compounds have no effect on bromine water (i.e. it stays brown).
- Instruments can be used to identify elements and compounds.

(HT) Empirical formula of a compound can be calculated by burning some of the substance in oxygen and measuring the mass of each product.

Unit 3 Practice Questions

1. The following statements relate to the modern periodic table of elements. Write down true or false next to each statement, as appropriate.

   a) The elements are arranged in order of their electronic structures. _____

   b) A group is a horizontal row of elements in the periodic table. _____

   c) Elements in the same group have different numbers of electrons in their outer shell. _____

   d) Metals are found on the right of the table. _____

   e) The electron configuration of oxygen is 2,6 and oxygen is in group 6. _____

2. Match the statements A, B, C and D with the chemicals 1 to 4 below.

   A   The alkali formed when potassium reacts with water. _____

   B   The gas formed when an alkali metal reacts with water. _____

   C   The chemical formed when chlorine gas is added to potassium iodide. _____

   D   The halogen that is a liquid at room temperature. _____

   1 Potassium chloride   **2** Potassium hydroxide   **3** Bromine   **4** Hydrogen

3. a) Give two properties of transition metals.

   i) _____   ii) _____

   b) Give two uses of transition metals.

   i) _____   ii) _____

4. Which accurate technique can be used to find out how much of an acid is needed to neutralise a certain volume of alkali?

   _____

5. a) Give the definition of a strong acid.

   _____

   HT b) A weak acid is used to neutralise a strong alkali. Which indicator should be used?

HT 6 $0.01\,dm^3$ hydrochloric acid neutralises $0.05\,dm^3$ sodium hydroxide solution which has a concentration of $2\,mol\,dm^{-3}$. Calculate the concentration of the hydrochloric acid used.

7 This question is about the solubility of the compound potassium nitrate (KNO_3).

a) How many grams of potassium nitrate per 100g water are needed to make a saturated solution at 40°C?

b) If a saturated solution of potassium nitrate is cooled from 60°C to 40°C, how many grams of potassium nitrate per 100g water will crystallise out?

8 Write hard or soft next to each of the statements below to indicate whether they relate to hard water or soft water.

a) It reacts with soap to form a scum.

b) It is made when tap water is passed through an ion exchange column containing hydrogen or sodium ions.

c) When heated, it produces scale that can reduce the efficiency of heating systems or kettles.

d) It contains dissolved compounds of calcium and magnesium.

9 Draw and label an energy level diagram which shows the energy change which takes place in an exothermic reaction.

Glossary of Key Words

Acid – a compound that has a pH lower than 7.

Activation energy – the minimum amount of energy required to cause a reaction.

Additive – a substance added to food to make it last longer or to improve flavour, appearance, etc.

Alkali – a compound that has a pH higher than 7.

Alkane – a saturated hydrocarbon with the general formula C_nH_{2n+2}

Alkene – an unsaturated hydrocarbon (with at least one double carbon carbon bond) with the general formula C_nH_{2n}

Alloy – a mixture of two or more metals, or a mixture of one metal and a non-metal.

Atom – the smallest part of an element which can enter into a chemical reaction.

Atom economy – a measure of the amount of reactants in a chemical reaction which end up as useful products; usually expressed as a percentage.

Atomic number – the number of protons in an atom.

Calorie (C) – unit of energy (equal to 4.2 joules).

Catalyst – a substance that increases the rate of a chemical reaction without being changed itself.

Chemical formula – a way of showing the elements that are present in molecules of a substance.

Chemical reaction – a process in which one or more substances are changed into others.

Chromatography – a technique used to separate different compounds in a mixture according to how well they dissolve a particular solvent.

Compound – a substance consisting of two or more elements chemically combined together.

Conductor – a substance that readily transfers heat or energy.

Covalent bond – a bond between two atoms, in which both atoms share one or more electrons.

Covalent compound – compound formed when two (or more) elements bond covalently.

Cracking – the process used to break down long-chain hydrocarbons into more useful short-chain hydrocarbons, using high temperatures and a catalyst.

Crude oil – a liquid mixture found in rocks, which contains hydrocarbons.

Current – the flow of electric charge through a conductor.

Decomposition – breaking down.

Dissociate – separate.

Distillation – a process of separating a liquid mixture by boiling it and condensing its vapours.

Efficiency – the energy output expressed as a percentage of energy input.

Electrodes – pieces of metal or carbon which allow electric current to enter and leave during electrolysis.

Electrolysis – the process by which an electric current causes a solution to undergo chemical decomposition.

Electron – a negatively charged subatomic particle that orbits the nucleus.

Electronic structure – the arrangement of electrons around the nucleus of an atom.

Element – a substance that consists of only one type of atom.

Emulsion – a mixture of oil and water.

Endothermic – a reaction that takes in heat from its surroundings.

Energy – the ability to do work; measured in joules (J).

Evidence – observations, measurements and data collected and subjected to some form of validation.

Exothermic – a reaction that gives out heat to its surroundings.

Fossil – the remains of animals / plants preserved in rock.

Fossil fuel – fuel formed in the ground, over millions of years, from the remains of dead plants and animals.

Fractional distillation – the process used to separate crude oil into groups of hydrocarbons whose molecules have a similar number of carbon atoms.

Fuel – a substance that releases heat or energy when combined with oxygen.

Global warming – the increase in the average temperature on Earth due to a rise in the levels of greenhouse gases in the atmosphere.

Hydrocarbon – a compound containing only hydrogen and carbon.

Hydrogenation – the process in which hydrogen is used to harden vegetable oils.

Insoluble – a substance that will not dissolve in a solvent.

Ion – a charged particle formed when an atom gains or loses electrons.

Ionic bond – the bond formed between two (or more) atoms when one loses, and another gains, electrons to become charged ions.

Ionic compound – a compound formed when two (or more) elements bond ionically.

Isotopes – atoms of the same element which contain different numbers of neutrons.

Joule (J) – a unit of energy.

Mass number – the total number of protons and neutrons present in an atom.

Minerals – naturally occurring chemical elements and compounds found in rocks.

Mole (mol) – the molar mass of a substance, i.e. the mass in grams of 6×10^{23} particles.

Nanoscience – dealing with materials that have a very small grain size, in the order of 1–100nm.

Neutralisation – a reaction between an acid and a base which forms a neutral solution (i.e. pH7).

Neutron – a subatomic particle found in the nucleus of an atom which has no charge.

Non-biodegradable – a substance that does not decompose naturally by the action of microorganisms.

Nucleus – the small central core of an atom, consisting of protons and neutrons.

Obesity – the condition of being very overweight.

Ore – a naturally occurring mineral, from which it is economically viable to extract a metal.

Oxidation – a reaction involving the gain of oxygen, the loss of hydrogen, or the loss of electrons.

pH – a measure of acidity or alkalinity.

Pollution – the contamination of an environment by chemicals, waste or heat.

Polymer – a giant, long-chained hydrocarbon.

Polymerisation – the process of monomers joining together to form a polymer.

Precipitate – an insoluble solid formed in a precipitation reaction.

Products – the substances made at the end of a chemical reaction.

Proton – a positively charged subatomic particle found in the nucleus.

Reactants – the substances present before a chemical reaction takes place.

Reduction – a reaction involving the loss of oxygen, the gain of hydrogen, or the gain of electrons.

Relative formula mass (M_r) – the sum of the atomic masses of all atoms in a molecule.

Reversible reaction – a reaction in which products can react to reform the original reactants.

Glossary of Key Words

Salt – the product of a chemical reaction between a base and an acid.

Saturated (i.e. a solution) – a solution in which no more solute can be dissolved at a particular temperature.

Sedimentary rock – rock formed by the accumulation of sediment.

Smart alloy – an alloy which can change shape and then return to its original shape.

Smart materials – materials which have one or more properties that can be altered.

Solubility – the ability of a substance to dissolve in a solvent.

Soluble – a substance that can dissolve in a solvent.

Solute – the substance that dissolves in a solvent.

Solvent – the substance that dissolves the solute.

Sustainable – resources that can be replaced.

Tectonic plates – huge sections of the Earth's crust which move in relation to one another.

Theory – the best way to explain why something is happening. It can be changed when new evidence is found.

Thermal energy – heat energy.

Titration – a method used to find the concentration of an acid or alkali.

Tsunami – a huge tidal wave caused by an earthquake under the sea.

(HT) **Equilibrium** – the state in which a chemical reaction proceeds at the same rate as its reverse reaction (the reactants are balanced).

Relative atomic mass (A_r) – the average mass of an atom of an element compared with a twelfth of the mass of a carbon atom.

Yield – the amount of a product obtained from a reaction.

Acknowledgements

The author and publisher would like to thank everyone who has contributed to this book:

p.10 © iStockphoto.com / Peter Galbraith
p.17 © iStockphoto.com / Julie Felton

Author: Christine Horbury

Project Editor: Rachael Hemsley

Cover Design: Angela English

Concept Design: Sarah Duxbury and Helen Jacobs

Designer: Nicola Lancashire

Artwork: HL Studios and Lonsdale.

Author Information

Christine Horbury is a science consultant for an LEA. She works closely with the exam boards and has an excellent understanding of the new science specifications, which she is helping to implement in local schools.

As a former science teacher, with over 30 years' experience, her main objective in writing this book was to produce a user-friendly revision guide for students, which would also act as a useful reference for teachers. As such, this guide provides full coverage of all the essential material, cross-referenced to the specification for ease of use and presented in a clear and interesting manner that is accessible to everyone.

Answers to Practice Questions

Unit 1a

1. A 4; B 1; C 2; D 3.
2. **a)** ii) calcium carbonate
   b) iv) quicklime and carbon dioxide
   c) i) slaked lime
3. A 2; B 4; C 1; D 3.
4. Gold is unreactive and is found in the Earth as the metal itself.
5. **a)** The metal oxide is heated with carbon. The reaction produces lead and carbon dioxide.
   b) Lead is below carbon in the reactivity series. Carbon will displace less reactive metals from their oxides.
6. **a)** Electrolysis.
   b) Aluminium is above carbon in the reactivity series and, therefore, reduction will not work.

7. **a)–b) Any two from:** Saves energy; Less pollution; Metal ores are becoming less plentiful; Less damage to the environment.
8. A 4; B 3; C 2; D 1.
9.

$$H-\overset{\displaystyle H}{\underset{\displaystyle H}{\overset{|}{\underset{|}{C}}}}-\overset{\displaystyle H}{\underset{\displaystyle H}{\overset{|}{\underset{|}{C}}}}-H$$

10. **a)** Its boiling point will be higher.
    b) Its viscosity will increase (it will flow less easily).
11. **a)** Carbon dioxide (CO_2) and water (H_2O).
    b) Sulfur dioxide (SO_2).
    c) $S + O_2 \longrightarrow SO_2$

Unit 1b

1. A 4; B 3; C 1; D 2.
2. A 2; B 3; C 4; D 1.
3. **a)** iii) monomers
   b) iii)

$$\left(\overset{\displaystyle |}{\underset{\displaystyle |}{C}} = \overset{\displaystyle |}{\underset{\displaystyle |}{C}} \right)_n$$

   c) iv) transparent and flexible
4. **a)–b) In any order:** Pressing (squeezing); Distillation.
5. **a)** By mixing oil and water.
   b) Emulsions are thicker than oil and water.
6. Bromine water is decolorised by an unsaturated fat / oil.

7.

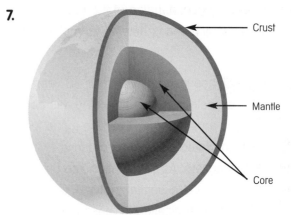

8. **a)** Closely matching coastlines. Similar patterns of rocks, containing fossils of the same plants and animals.
   b) **i)–ii) Any two from:** Plates slide past each other; Plates move towards each other; Plates move away from each other.
9. **a)–b) Any two from:** Earthquakes; Volcanic eruptions; Tsunamis.
10. A 3; B 4; C 1; D 2.

Unit 2

1. **a)** i) Electron
   b) iv) 12
   c) i) Group 1
   d) i) Positive
2. **a)** The reaction is reversible.
   b) It means that heat (energy) is given out.
   c) **Nitrogen**: from the air (atmosphere); **Hydrogen**: from natural gas.
   d) There are more moles of reactants than products, i.e. 4 molecules of reactants are changed into 2 molecules of product
   e) **i)** Iron
   ii) To speed up the reaction.
3. **a)** Relative formula mass = 23 + 16 +1 = 40.
   b) $\frac{16}{40}$ x 100 = 40%.
   c) $\frac{40}{100}$ x 5 = 2g.
   d) 1 mole of NaOH = 23 + 16 + 1 = 40g.
   4 moles of NaOH = 40 x 4 = **160g**

4. **a)** Each carbon atom forms four strong covalent bonds with other carbon atoms.
   b) Very high melting points.
5. **a)** Chlorine
   b) The ions are positively charged and they are attracted to the negative (oppositely charged) electrode.
   c) Reduction is the gain of electrons and oxidation is the loss of electrons.
6. **a)** **i)** Potassium chloride
   ii) Sulfuric acid
   iii) Sodium hydroxide
   iv) Barium sulfate + zinc chloride
   b) Barium sulfate

Unit 3

1. **a)** True
   b) False
   c) False
   d) False
   e) True
2. A 2; B 4; C 1; D 3
3. **a)** **i)–ii) Any two from:** Form coloured compounds; Have ions with different charges; Are good conductors of heat and electricity; Can be easily bent or hammered into shape.
   b) **i)–ii)** As catalysts; and any sensible answer.
4. Titration
5. **a)** One which is completely ionised in water.
   b) Phenolphthalein
6. $10\,mol\,dm^{-3}$

7. **a)** 27g
   b) 11g
8. **a)** Hard
   b) Soft
   c) Hard
   d) Hard
9.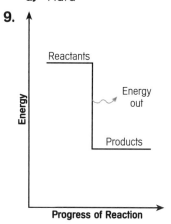

Index

Periodic Table

Key

| relative atomic mass |
| **atomic symbol** |
| name |
| atomic (proton) number |

Example:

| 1 |
| **H** |
| hydrogen |
| 1 |

1	2											3	4	5	6	7	8 or 0
																	4 **He** helium 2
7 **Li** lithium 3	9 **Be** beryllium 4											11 **B** boron 5	12 **C** carbon 6	14 **N** nitrogen 7	16 **O** oxygen 8	19 **F** fluorine 9	20 **Ne** neon 10
23 **Na** sodium 11	24 **Mg** magnesium 12											27 **Al** aluminium 13	28 **Si** silicon 14	31 **P** phosphorus 15	32 **S** sulfur 16	35.5 **Cl** chlorine 17	40 **Ar** argon 18
39 **K** potassium 19	40 **Ca** calcium 20	45 **Sc** scandium 21	48 **Ti** titanium 22	51 **V** vanadium 23	52 **Cr** chromium 24	55 **Mn** manganese 25	56 **Fe** iron 26	59 **Co** cobalt 27	59 **Ni** nickel 28	63.5 **Cu** copper 29	65 **Zn** zinc 30	70 **Ga** gallium 31	73 **Ge** germanium 32	75 **As** arsenic 33	79 **Se** selenium 34	80 **Br** bromine 35	84 **Kr** krypton 36
85 **Rb** rubidium 37	88 **Sr** strontium 38	89 **Y** yttrium 39	91 **Zr** zirconium 40	93 **Nb** niobium 41	96 **Mo** molybdenum 42	[98] **Tc** technetium 43	101 **Ru** ruthenium 44	103 **Rh** rhodium 45	106 **Pd** palladium 46	108 **Ag** silver 47	112 **Cd** cadmium 48	115 **In** indium 49	119 **Sn** tin 50	122 **Sb** antimony 51	128 **Te** tellurium 52	127 **I** iodine 53	131 **Xe** xenon 54
133 **Cs** caesium 55	137 **Ba** barium 56	139 **La*** lanthanum 57	178 **Hf** hafnium 72	181 **Ta** tantalum 73	184 **W** tungsten 74	186 **Re** rhenium 75	190 **Os** osmium 76	192 **Ir** iridium 77	195 **Pt** platinum 78	197 **Au** gold 79	201 **Hg** mercury 80	204 **Tl** thallium 81	207 **Pb** lead 82	209 **Bi** bismuth 83	[209] **Po** polonium 84	[210] **At** astatine 85	[222] **Rn** radon 86
[223] **Fr** francium 87	[226] **Ra** radium 88	[227] **Ac*** actinium 89	[261] **Rf** rutherfordium 104	[262] **Db** dubnium 105	[266] **Sg** seaborgium 106	[264] **Bh** bohrium 107	[277] **Hs** hassium 108	[268] **Mt** meitnerium 109	[271] **Ds** darmstadtium 110	[272] **Rg** roentgenium 111							

Elements which have atomic numbers 112–116 have been reported but not fully authenticated.

*The Lanthanides (atomic numbers 58–71) and the Actinides (atomic numbers 90–103) have been omitted.

Cu and Cl have not been rounded to the nearest whole number.

→ The lines of elements going across are called **periods**.

→ The columns of elements going down are called **groups**.